The Complete Instant Vortex Dual Basket Air Fryer Cookbook

1500 Days of Affordable, Easy, Delicious Vortex Dual Basket Air Fryer Recipes, Your Best Companion (2023)

Rachel R. Donlon

Copyright © 2023 by Rachel R. Donlon - All rights reserved.

The content contained within this book may not be reproduced, duplicated, or transmitted without direct written permission from the author or the publisher. Under no circumstances will any blame or legal responsibility be held against the publisher, or author, for any damages, reparation, or monetary loss due to the information contained within this book, either directly or indirectly.

Legal Notice: This book is copyright protected. It is only for personal use. You cannot amend, distribute, sell, use, quote or paraphrase any part, or the content within this book, without the consent of the author or publisher.

Disclaimer Notice: Please note the information contained within this document is for educational and entertainment purposes only. All effort has been executed to present accurate, up to date, reliable, complete information. No warranties of any kind are declared or implied. Readers acknowledge that the author is not engaged in the rendering of legal, financial, medical, or professional advice. The content within this book has been derived from various sources. Please consult a licensed professional before attempting any techniques outlined in this book. By reading this document, the reader agrees that under no circumstances is the author responsible for any losses, direct or indirect, that are incurred as a result of the use of the information contained within this document, including, but not limited to, errors, omissions, or inaccuracies.

CONTENTS

INTRODUCTION 9
- How to Use the Instant Vortex Dual Basket Air Fryer 9
- Tips for Getting the Most Out of the Instant Vortex Dual Basket Air Fryer 10
- Air Frying vs Deep Frying 10

Bread And Breakfast Recipes 11
- Grit And Ham Fritters 11
- Parmesan Spinach Muffins 12
- Mozzarella Chives Omelet 12
- Spinach And Mushroom Mini Quiche 13
- Sourdough Croutons 13
- Tomato And Mozzarella Bruschetta 14
- Soufflé 14
- Baked Eggs 15
- Cranberry Beignets 15
- Homemade Cherry Breakfast Tarts 16
- French Toast Sticks With Strawberry Sauce 16
- Parmesan Sausage Egg Muffins 17
- Hearty Blueberry Oatmeal 17
- Cheddar Bacon Frittata 18
- Chicken Casserole With Almonds 18
- Baked Potato Breakfast Boats 19
- Paprika Zucchini Spread 19
- Creamy Baked Sausage 20
- Crispy Parmesan Asparagus 20
- Mixed Pepper Hash With Mozzarella Cheese 21
- Egg Soufflé With Mushroom And Broccoli 21
- Yogurt Eggs With Chives 22

Appetizers And Snacks Recipes 22

    Root Veggie Chips With Herb Salt 22

    Enticing Pork Meatballs 23

    Broccoli-spinach Dip 23

    Honey-glazed Chicken Drumettes 24

    Crispy Mustard Fried Leek 25

    Roasted Almonds With Paprika 25

    Apple Chips 26

    Spicy Chickpeas 26

    Delectable Chaffles 27

    Cajun Zucchini Chips 27

    Fried Bacon Slices 28

    Artichoke-spinach Dip 28

    Air Fried Shrimp & Bacon 29

    Roasted Buttery Cashews 29

    Corn With Coriander And Parmesan Cheese 30

    Buffalo Breaded Cauliflower Bites 30

    Crispy Old Bay Chicken Wings 31

    Breaded Artichoke Hearts 31

    Peppery Chicken Meatballs 32

    Spinach And Artichoke Dip Wontons 32

    Salmon Nachos 33

    Cheese Sticks With Coconut 33

Poultry Recipes 34

    Parmesan Chicken Wings 34

    Spicy Asian Chicken Thighs With Soy Sauce 34

    Marjoram Chicken Drumsticks 35

    Spice Chicken Pieces 35

    Honey Turkey Tenderloin 36

    Lemon Parmesan Chicken 36

    Cheesy Chicken Tacos 37

    Chicken & Mushroom Meatballs 37

    Italian Chicken And Veggies 38

    Potato Cheese Crusted Chicken 38

    Chicken And Vegetable Fajitas 39

    Breaded Homestyle Chicken Strips 40

Spice Chicken Wings With Parmesan Cheese 40
Tasty Chicken Fajitas 41
Tex-mex Turkey Burgers 41
Creamy Chicken Breasts With Jalapeno 42
Awesome Duck With Potato Rösti 42
Easy Tandoori Chicken 43
Spice Chicken With Broccoli 43
Roasted Chicken And Vegetable Salad 44
Crispy Chicken Cordon Bleu 44
Crispy Chicken And Pickles Sandwich 45

Beef, Pork & Lamb Recipes 46

Authentic Greek Vegetable Skillet 46
Juicy Cheeseburger 46
Beef And Spinach Rolls 47
Cheese Crusted Chops 47
Homemade And Delectable Pork Chops 48
Simple Pork Chops 48
Steak Fajitas With Vegetables 49
Unique Beef Cheeseburgers 49
Beef Bites With Potatoes 50
Korean Short Ribs 50
Italian Lamb Chops With Avocado Mayo 51
Cheesy Pork Chops 51
Pork Tenderloins 52
Peppercorn Crusted Beef Tenderloin 52
Beef And Mushroom Calzones 53
Air Fried Ribeye Steak 54
Beef Steak Fingers 54
Air Fried Beef Ribs 55
Cheesy Beef Meatballs 55
Sweet-and-sour Polish Sausage 56
Barbecued Baby Back Ribs 56
Beef With Spanish Rice Casserole 57

Fish And Seafood Recipes 58
- Flavor Moroccan Harissa Shrimp 58
- Sesame-glazed Salmon 58
- Cajun Lemon Branzino 59
- Tuna And Fruit Kebabs 59
- Creamy Savory Salmon 60
- Fish Mania With Mustard 60
- Old Bay Cod Fish Fillets 61
- Trimmed Mackerel With Spring Onions 61
- Spiced Catfish Fillets 62
- Clams With Spring Onions 62
- Cilantro-lime Fried Shrimp 63
- Pesto Fish Finger Sandwich 63
- Salmon Patties 64
- Glazed Fillets 64
- Lemon-pepper Tilapia With Garlic Aioli 65
- Red Snapper With Hot Chili Paste 65
- Beer Squid 66
- Garlic Shrimp 66
- Salmon On Bed Of Fennel And Carrot 67
- Baked Sardines 67
- Tasty Juicy Salmon 68
- Sea Bream Fillet With Tomato Sauce 68

Vegetarians Recipes 69
- Rice & Bean Burritos 69
- Hearty Salad 69
- Black Bean Empanadas 70
- Cheesy Enchilada Stuffed Baked Potatoes 71
- Vegetarian Stuffed Bell Peppers 72
- Black Bean Stuffed Potato Boats 72
- Meatless Kimchi Bowls 73
- Crispy Avocados With Pico De Gallo 73
- Corn On The Cob 74
- Gorgeous Jalapeño Poppers 74
- Pizza Portobello Mushrooms 75
- Broccoli Cheddar Stuffed Potatoes 76

Quinoa Burgers With Feta Cheese And Dill 77

Sweet Roasted Carrots 78

Cheddar Bean Taquitos 78

Basil Green Beans 78

Home-style Cinnamon Rolls 79

Cheesy Veggie Frittata 79

Party Giant Nachos 80

Garlicky Roasted Mushrooms 80

Quick-to-make Quesadillas 81

General Tso's Cauliflower 81

Vegetable Side Dishes Recipes 82

Cheddar Tomatillos With Lettuce 82

Potato With Creamy Cheese 82

Balsamic Brussels Sprouts 83

Roasted Brown Butter Carrots 83

Air Fried Brussels Sprouts 84

Spiced Cauliflower Medley 84

Herbed Radishes 85

Garlic Brussel Sprouts With Celery 85

Lush Summer Rolls 86

Parmesan Green Beans 86

Roasted Eggplant Slices 87

Crunchy Green Beans 87

Crispy Broccoli 88

Italian Eggplant And Tomato Bites 88

Garlic Kale Mash 89

Parmesan Zucchini Gratin 89

Spicy Sweet Potatoes 90

Balsamic Greens And Green Beans Medley 90

Yellow Squash Chips With Parmesan 91

Zucchini Tots With Mozzarella 91

Roasted "everything Bagel" Broccolini 92

Black Bean And Tomato Chili 92

Desserts And Sweets Recipes 93

Choco Chips Cookies With Macadamia Nuts 93
Graham Cracker Cheesecake 93
Chocolate-almond Candies 94
Sweet Orange Muffins 94
Chocolate Almond Cake 95
Chocolate Croissants 95
Strawberry Muffins With Cinnamon 96
Black Forest Pies 96
Mixed Berry Crumble 97
Berry Crumble 97
Cinnamon And Pecan Pie 98
Buttery Shortbread Sticks 98
Aromatic Cup With Blondies 99
Fried Bananas With Chocolate Sauce 99
Donuts With Cardamom 100
Sweet Blackberry Cream 100
Enticing Cappuccino Muffins 101
Vanilla Bars With Sesame Seeds 101
Spice Cookies 102
Fried Oreos 102
Cardamom And Vanilla Custard 103
Caramelized Peaches With Blueberries 103

Recipe Index 104

INTRODUCTION

Hi food lovers, thank you for purchasing my recipe book!

I'm Kendra C. Cannon, a food journalist and author who writes about food politics, cooking and nutrition. I often share my thoughts on life, love, and food on my blog, and I also love recipe experimentation and food photography. I grew up with a passion for cooking, first learning it from my father who was the head chef in the family. My dad is also the author of "How to Cook Everything" and has written for the New York Times for over 20 years. Influenced by him, I majored in nutrition and health at university, and now I am doing a job I like.

Other than that I travel a lot to different countries and my adventurous side is not limited to trying weird new recipes or exotic foods, often being inspired to take my taste buds home and recreate the wonderful things I just experienced new foods and tastes.

In this book, we focus on sharing low-fat, low-oil air fryer recipes, many of which are also vegetarian-friendly. Whether you're a low-fat meat eater, flexitarian, vegetarian, vegan, or following a gluten-free and/or dairy-free diet, you're sure to find a recipe to suit your tastes.

You will find a variety of delicious and easy recipes: delicious breakfast recipes, crispy air fryer chicken wings, juicy beef, pork and lamb recipes, mouth-watering fish and seafood recipes, delicious vegetarian and vegetable recipes, A wide variety of dessert recipes and more.

How to Use the Instant Vortex Dual Basket Air Fryer

The Instant Vortex Dual Basket Air Fryer is a versatile and convenient device that allows you to enjoy your favorite fried foods in a healthy way. With its large capacity, digital display and preset cooking functions, it's easy to cook a variety of foods to crispy perfection. It cooks food quickly and evenly. You can expect your food to be cooked to crispy perfection in a fraction of the time it takes in a conventional oven.

Using the Instant Vortex Double Basket Air Fryer is easy. First, you need to select the desired cooking function and set the temperature and cooking time using the digital display and touch controls. Then, place the food in the basket, which is then placed in the air fryer. The air fryer will start cooking the food using Rapid Air Technology.

Tips for Getting the Most Out of the Instant Vortex Dual Basket Air Fryer

Here are some things you can do to get the most out of your Instant Vortex Double Basket Air Fryer:

Preheating the Air Fryer: To ensure your food cooks evenly, it is best to preheat the air fryer before adding food. This will help the air fryer reach the desired temperature faster, resulting in better-cooked food.

Less or No Oil: One of the benefits of using an air fryer is that you can enjoy fried foods with little or no oil. For the crispiest results, you may want to lightly coat the food with oil or cooking spray.

Shake the Basket: Cook in batches for faster, better air fryer food. Air fryer cooking is usually faster than baking or frying. So don't stress about cooking everything at once! To ensure your food cooks evenly, it is best to shake the basket halfway through the cooking time. This will help the hot air circulate more evenly around the food.

Experiment with different cooking times and temperatures: The Instant Vortex Dual Basket Air Fryer has a variety of cooking temperatures and times, so you can experiment to find the perfect setting for your favorite foods.

Foods are a good size: eg keep vegetables 1/4 inch wide to keep them from falling over. The width of thick cut french fries is the perfect width for food that won't fall through the cracks in the basket and still cook quickly. Make sweet potatoes, vegetables, etc. at least 1/4 inch wide so they stay in the basket.

Air Frying vs Deep Frying

Dig into a serving of french fries or a plate of fried chicken and the pleasure hits you right away -- that familiar, crispy crunch and moist, chewy center.

But the appealing taste of fried foods comes at a cost. Research links the oils used to cook them to health problems like heart disease, type 2 diabetes, and cancer.

Enter the Air Fryer - the appliance that guarantees the taste, texture, and golden brownness of deep-fried foods, without more fat and calories.

When we looked at the difference between frying and air frying, there was one clear winner (hint: it's air frying!). The main reason why air frying is more popular than deep frying has to do with the amount of oil used. Fryers need a few liters of oil, air fryers don't!

Eating too much fried food can easily lead to overeating. That said, air frying significantly reduces the amount of oil absorbed by food compared to deep frying. This is a benefit of using an air fryer, as less oil generally results in fewer calories consumed, which can reduce the risk of weight gain, obesity, and more.

If you prefer to eat fried food, then the air fryer is definitely a good choice. Still, the air fryer isn't a magic machine for making any food definitively "healthy." If you usually cook food in the oven, an air fryer can be a great tool to add more variety to your cooking!

Bread And Breakfast Recipes

Grit And Ham Fritters

Servings: 8
Cooking Time: 20 Minutes

Ingredients:

- 4 cups water
- 1 cup quick-cooking grits
- ¼ teaspoon salt
- 2 tablespoons butter
- 2 cups grated Cheddar cheese, divided
- 1 cup finely diced ham
- 1 tablespoon chopped chives
- Salt and freshly ground black pepper, to taste
- 1 egg, beaten
- 2 cups panko bread crumbs
- Cooking spray

Directions:

1. Bring the water to a boil in a saucepan. Whisk in the grits and ¼ teaspoon of salt, and cook for 7 minutes until the grits are soft. Remove the pan from the heat and stir in the butter and 1 cup of the grated Cheddar cheese. Transfer the grits to a bowl and let them cool for 10 to 15 minutes.
2. Stir the ham, chives and the rest of the cheese into the grits and season with salt and pepper to taste. Add the beaten egg and refrigerate the mixture for 30 minutes.
3. Put the panko bread crumbs in a shallow dish. Measure out ¼-cup portions of the grits mixture and shape them into patties. Coat all sides of the patties with the panko bread crumbs, patting them with the hands so the crumbs adhere to the patties. You should have about 16 patties. Spritz both sides of the patties with cooking spray.
4. Preheat the air fryer to 400°F (204°C).
5. In batches of 5 or 6, air fry the fritters for 8 minutes. Using a flat spatula, flip the fritters over and air fry for another 4 minutes.

Parmesan Spinach Muffins

Servings: 4
Cooking Time: 15 Minutes
Ingredients:
- 2 eggs, whisked
- Cooking spray
- 1 and ½ cups coconut milk
- 1 tablespoon baking powder
- 4 ounces baby spinach, chopped
- 2 ounces parmesan cheese, grated
- 3 ounces almond flour

Directions:
1. Grease the muffin molds with cooking spray.
2. Mix the whisked eggs, coconut milk, baking powder, baby spinach, parmesan cheese, and almond flour together in a mixing bowl.
3. Transfer onto the greased molds.
4. Cook in your air fryer at 380 degrees F/ 195 degrees C for 15 minutes.
5. When the cooking time is up, serve on plates.
6. Enjoy your breakfast.

Mozzarella Chives Omelet

Servings: 4
Cooking Time: 20 Minutes
Ingredients:
- 6 eggs, whisked
- 1 cup chives, chopped
- Cooking spray
- 1 cup mozzarella, shredded
- Salt and black pepper to the taste

Directions:
1. Grease a suitable baking pan with cooking spray.
2. Mix the whisked eggs, chopped chives, shredded mozzarella, salt, and black pepper in a medium bowl.
3. Pour the egg mixture onto the greased pan and spread.
4. Cook in your air fryer at 350 degrees F/ 175 degrees C for 20 minutes.
5. When cooked, serve on plates.

Spinach And Mushroom Mini Quiche

Servings: 4
Cooking Time: 15 Minutes

Ingredients:
- 1 teaspoon olive oil, plus more for spraying
- 1 cup coarsely chopped mushrooms
- 1 cup fresh baby spinach, shredded
- 4 eggs, beaten
- ½ cup shredded Cheddar cheese
- ½ cup shredded mozzarella cheese
- ¼ teaspoon salt
- ¼ teaspoon black pepper

Directions:
1. Spray 4 silicone baking cups with olive oil and set aside.
2. In a medium sauté pan over medium heat, warm 1 teaspoon of olive oil. Add the mushrooms and sauté until soft, 3 to 4 minutes.
3. Add the spinach and cook until wilted, 1 to 2 minutes. Set aside.
4. In a medium bowl, whisk together the eggs, Cheddar cheese, mozzarella cheese, salt, and pepper.
5. Gently fold the mushrooms and spinach into the egg mixture.
6. Pour ¼ of the mixture into each silicone baking cup.
7. Place the baking cups into the fryer basket and air fry for 5 minutes. Stir the mixture in each ramekin slightly and air fry until the egg has set, an additional 3 to 5 minutes.

Sourdough Croutons

Servings: 4
Cooking Time: 6 Minutes

Ingredients:
- 4 cups cubed sourdough bread, 1-inch cubes
- 1 tablespoon olive oil
- 1 teaspoon fresh thyme leaves
- ¼ teaspoon salt
- Freshly ground black pepper, to taste

Directions:
1. Combine all ingredients in a bowl.
2. Preheat the air fryer to 400°F (204°C).
3. Toss the bread cubes into the air fryer and air fry for 6 minutes, shaking the basket once or twice while they cook.
4. Serve warm.

Tomato And Mozzarella Bruschetta

Servings: 1
Cooking Time: 4 Minutes
Ingredients:
- 6 small loaf slices
- ½ cup tomatoes, finely chopped
- 3 ounces (85 g) Mozzarella cheese, grated
- 1 tablespoon fresh basil, chopped
- 1 tablespoon olive oil

Directions:
1. Preheat the air fryer to 350°F (177°C).
2. Put the loaf slices inside the air fryer and air fry for about 3 minutes.
3. Add the tomato, Mozzarella, basil, and olive oil on top.
4. Air fry for an additional minute before serving.

Soufflé

Servings: 4
Cooking Time: 22 Minutes
Ingredients:
- ⅓ cup butter, melted
- ¼ cup flour
- 1 cup milk
- 1 ounce (28 g) sugar
- 4 egg yolks
- 1 teaspoon vanilla extract
- 6 egg whites
- 1 teaspoon cream of tartar
- Cooking spray

Directions:
1. In a bowl, mix the butter and flour until a smooth consistency is achieved.
2. Pour the milk into a saucepan over medium-low heat. Add the sugar and allow to dissolve before raising the heat to boil the milk.
3. Pour in the flour and butter mixture and stir rigorously for 7 minutes to eliminate any lumps. Make sure the mixture thickens. Take off the heat and allow to cool for 15 minutes.
4. Preheat the air fryer to 320°F (160°C). Spritz 6 soufflé dishes with cooking spray.
5. Put the egg yolks and vanilla extract in a separate bowl and beat them together with a fork. Pour in the milk and combine well to incorporate everything.
6. In a smaller bowl mix the egg whites and cream of tartar with a fork. Fold into the egg yolks-milk mixture before adding in the flour mixture. Transfer equal amounts to the 6 soufflé dishes.
7. Put the dishes in the air fryer and bake for 15 minutes.
8. Serve warm.

Baked Eggs

Servings: 3
Cooking Time: 10 Minutes
Ingredients:
- 3 eggs
- ½ teaspoon ground turmeric
- ¼ teaspoon salt
- 3 bacon slices
- 1 teaspoon butter, melted

Directions:
1. Using the ½ teaspoon of melted butter, grease the silicone muffin molds.
2. Place the bacon slices on the molds, shaped into circles.
3. Before cooking, heat your air fryer to 400 degrees F/ 205 degrees C.
4. Cook the bacon inside the preheated air fryer for 7 minutes.
5. When cooked, with the remaining butter brush the center of the muffins.
6. Then crack in eggs in every bacon circles.
7. To season, sprinkle with ground turmeric and salt.
8. Cook again in your air fryer for 3 minutes or more.

Cranberry Beignets

Servings: 16
Cooking Time: 10 Minutes
Ingredients:
- 1½ cups flour
- 2 teaspoons baking soda
- ¼ teaspoon salt
- 3 tablespoons brown sugar
- ⅓ cup chopped dried cranberries
- ½ cup buttermilk
- 1 egg
- 3 tablespoons melted unsalted butter

Directions:
1. In a medium bowl, combine the flour, baking soda, salt, and brown sugar, and mix well. Stir in dried cranberries.
2. In a small bowl, combine the buttermilk and egg, and beat until smooth. Stir into the dry ingredients just until moistened.
3. Pat the dough into an 8-by-8-inch square and cut into 16 pieces. Coat each piece lightly with melted butter.
4. Place in a single layer in the air fryer basket, making sure the pieces don't touch. You may have to cook in batches depending on the size of your air fryer basket. Air-fry for 5 to 8 minutes or until puffy and golden brown. Dust with powdered sugar before serving, if desired.
5. Did You Know? Using unsalted butter ensures food will not stick to the air fryer basket when cooking. Salt in butter can make foods stick, which is not what you want.

Homemade Cherry Breakfast Tarts

Servings: 6
Cooking Time: 20 Minutes
Ingredients:

- For the tarts
- 2 refrigerated piecrusts
- ⅓ cup cherry preserves
- 1 teaspoon cornstarch
- Cooking oil

- For the frosting
- ½ cup vanilla yogurt
- 1 ounce cream cheese
- 1 teaspoon stevia
- Rainbow sprinkles

Directions:
1. Place the piecrusts on a flat surface. Using a knife or pizza cutter, cut each piecrust into 3 rectangles, for 6 total. (I discard the unused dough left from slicing the edges.)
2. In a small bowl, combine the preserves and cornstarch. Mix well.
3. Scoop 1 tablespoon of the preserves mixture onto the top half of each piece of piecrust.
4. Fold the bottom of each piece up to close the tart. Using the back of a fork, press along the edges of each tart to seal.
5. Spray the breakfast tarts with cooking oil and place them in the air fryer. I do not recommend stacking the breakfast tarts. They will stick together if stacked. You may need to prepare them in two batches. Cook for 10 minutes.
6. Allow the breakfast tarts to cool fully before removing from the air fryer.
7. If necessary, repeat steps 5 and 6 for the remaining breakfast tarts.
8. In a small bowl, combine the yogurt, cream cheese, and stevia. Mix well.
9. Spread the breakfast tarts with frosting and top with sprinkles, and serve.

French Toast Sticks With Strawberry Sauce

Servings: 4
Cooking Time:10 To 14 Minutes
Ingredients:

- 3 slices low-sodium whole-wheat bread, each cut into 4 strips (see Tip)
- 1 tablespoon unsalted butter, melted
- 1 egg
- 1 egg white
- 1 tablespoon 2 percent milk
- 1 tablespoon sugar
- 1 cup sliced fresh strawberries
- 1 tablespoon freshly squeezed lemon juice

Directions:
1. Place the bread strips on a plate and drizzle with the melted butter.
2. In a shallow bowl, beat the egg, egg white, milk, and sugar.
3. Dip the bread into the egg mixture and place on a wire rack to let the batter drip off.
4. Air-fry half of the bread strips for 5 to 7 minutes, turning the strips with tongs once during cooking, until golden brown. Repeat with the remaining strips.
5. In a small bowl, mash the strawberries and lemon juice with a fork or potato masher. Serve the strawberry sauce with the French toast sticks.

Parmesan Sausage Egg Muffins

Servings: 4
Cooking Time: 20 Minutes

Ingredients:
- 6 ounces (170 g) Italian sausage, sliced
- 6 eggs
- ⅛ cup heavy cream
- Salt and ground black pepper, to taste
- 3 ounces (85 g) Parmesan cheese, grated

Directions:
1. Preheat the air fryer to 350°F (177°C). Grease a muffin pan.
2. Put the sliced sausage in the muffin pan.
3. Beat the eggs with the cream in a bowl and season with salt and pepper.
4. Pour half of the mixture over the sausages in the pan.
5. Sprinkle with cheese and the remaining egg mixture.
6. Bake in the preheated air fryer for 20 minutes or until set.
7. Serve immediately.

Hearty Blueberry Oatmeal

Servings: 6
Cooking Time: 25 Minutes

Ingredients:
- 1½ cups quick oats
- 1¼ teaspoons ground cinnamon, divided
- ½ teaspoon baking powder
- Pinch salt
- 1 cup unsweetened vanilla almond milk
- ¼ cup honey
- 1 teaspoon vanilla extract
- 1 egg, beaten
- 2 cups blueberries
- Olive oil
- 1½ teapoons sugar, divided
- 6 tablespoons low-fat whipped topping (optional)

Directions:
1. In a large bowl, mix together the oats, 1 teaspoon of cinnamon, baking powder, and salt.
2. In a medium bowl, whisk together the almond milk, honey, vanilla and egg.
3. Pour the liquid ingredients into the oats mixture and stir to combine. Fold in the blueberries.
4. Lightly spray a round air fryer–friendly pan with oil.
5. Add half the blueberry mixture to the pan.
6. Sprinkle ⅛ teaspoon of cinnamon and ½ teaspoon sugar over the top.
7. Cover the pan with aluminum foil and place gently in the fryer basket.
8. Air fry for 20 minutes. Remove the foil and air fry for an additional 5 minutes. Transfer the mixture to a shallow bowl.
9. Repeat with the remaining blueberry mixture, ½ teaspoon of sugar, and ⅛ teaspoon of cinnamon.
10. To serve, spoon into bowls and top with whipped topping.

Cheddar Bacon Frittata

Servings: 2
Cooking Time: 15 Minutes
Ingredients:
- ¼ cup green bell pepper, seeded and chopped
- 1 tablespoon olive oil
- ¼ cup spinach, chopped
- 2 bacon slices, chopped
- 4-6 cherry tomatoes, make halves
- 3 large eggs
- ¼ cup cheddar cheese, shredded

Directions:
1. On a flat kitchen surface, plug your air fryer and turn it on.
2. Preheat your air fryer for about 4-5 minutes to 360 degrees F/ 180 degrees C.
3. Gently coat your air frying basket with cooking oil or spray.
4. In a medium sized bowl, mix the tomatoes, bell pepper, and bacon thoroughly.
5. Place into the basket.
6. Transfer the basket in the air fryer. Let it cook for the next 8 minutes.
7. Mix thoroughly the spinach, cheese, and eggs in a medium sized bowl.
8. Remove the basket; Mix them together and cook for 8 more minutes.
9. Serve warm!

Chicken Casserole With Almonds

Servings: 4
Cooking Time: 25 Minutes
Ingredients:
- ¼ cup almonds, chopped
- ½ cup almond milk
- 4 eggs, whisked
- 1 cup chicken meat, cooked and shredded
- ½ teaspoon oregano, dried
- Cooking spray
- Salt and black pepper to the taste

Directions:
1. Grease a suitable baking pan with the cooking spray.
2. Mix the whisked eggs together with the rest ingredients in a medium bowl.
3. Pour the mixture onto the baking pan and spread
4. Cook in your air fryer at 350 degrees F/ 175 degrees C for 25 minutes.
5. When cooked, serve warm on plates.

Baked Potato Breakfast Boats

Servings: 4
Cooking Time: 20 Minutes
Ingredients:
- 2 large russet potatoes, scrubbed
- Olive oil
- Salt
- Freshly ground black pepper
- 4 eggs
- 2 tablespoons chopped, cooked bacon
- 1 cup shredded cheddar cheese

Directions:
1. Poke holes in the potatoes with a fork and microwave on full power for 5 minutes.
2. Turn potatoes over and cook an additional 3 to 5 minutes, or until the potatoes are fork tender.
3. Cut the potatoes in half lengthwise and use a spoon to scoop out the inside of the potato. Be careful to leave a layer of potato so that it makes a sturdy "boat."
4. Lightly spray the fryer basket with olive oil. Spray the skin side of the potatoes with oil and sprinkle with salt and pepper to taste.
5. Place the potato skins in the fryer basket skin side down. Crack one egg into each potato skin.
6. Sprinkle ½ tablespoon of bacon pieces and ¼ cup of shredded cheese on top of each egg. Sprinkle with salt and pepper to taste.
7. Air fry until the yolk is slightly runny, 5 to 6 minutes, or until the yolk is fully cooked, 7 to 10 minutes.

Paprika Zucchini Spread

Servings: 4
Cooking Time: 15 Minutes
Ingredients:
- 4 zucchinis, roughly chopped
- 1 tablespoon sweet paprika
- Salt and black pepper to the taste
- 1 tablespoon butter, melted

Directions:
1. Using butter, brush the bottom of a suitable baking pan.
2. Then add the rest ingredients in the baking pan.
3. Cook in your air fryer at 360 degrees F/ 180 degrees C for 15 minutes.
4. Transfer the cooked mixture to a blender and pulse well.
5. Serve into bowls and enjoy your breakfast.

Creamy Baked Sausage

Servings: 6
Cooking Time: 23 Minutes
Ingredients:
- 2 jalapeno peppers, sliced
- 7 ounces ground sausages
- 1 teaspoon dill seeds
- 3 ounces Colby Jack Cheese, shredded
- 4 eggs, beaten
- 1 tablespoon cream cheese
- ½ teaspoon salt
- 1 teaspoon butter, softened
- 1 teaspoon olive oil

Directions:
1. Before cooking, heat your skillet and then pour the olive oil inside the skillet.
2. Place salt and ground sausage in the skillet and cook for 5 to 8 minutes on medium heat.
3. During cooking, stir the mixture from time to time.
4. At the same time, heat your air fryer ahead of time to 400 degrees F/ 205 degrees C.
5. Using softened butter, grease your air fryer basket.
6. Transfer the cooked sausage inside the greased basket and flatten the mixture.
7. Sprinkle the sliced jalapeno pepper on the top of the mixture.
8. Then add shredded cheese.
9. In a second bowl, beat the eggs together and mix together with cream cheese.
10. Pour the egg-cheese mixture over the sausage mixture.
11. Sprinkle with dill seeds.
12. Cook the egg-cheese mixture in your air fryer at 400 degrees F/ 205 degrees C for 16 minutes.
13. If prefer a crunchy crust, cook for a few more minutes.

Crispy Parmesan Asparagus

Servings: 4
Cooking Time: 10 Minutes
Ingredients:
- 1 pound asparagus spears
- 2 tablespoons butter
- ½ cup Parmesan cheese, grated
- Salt/Black pepper
- 1 teaspoon lemon zest

Directions:
1. Prepare all the recipe ingredients. Peel the asparagus, wash and dry.
2. Season the asparagus spears with black pepper and salt and brush with butter.
3. Arrange them in a deep air fryer basket and cook at 370 degrees F/ 185 degrees C, for about 8 to 10 minutes. Shake a couple of times while cooking.
4. Serve with parmesan and lemon zest.

Mixed Pepper Hash With Mozzarella Cheese

Servings: 4
Cooking Time: 20 Minutes

Ingredients:

- 1 red bell pepper, cut into strips
- 1 green bell pepper, cut into strips
- 1 orange bell pepper, cut into strips
- 4 eggs, whisked
- Salt and black pepper to the taste
- 2 tablespoons mozzarella, shredded
- Cooking spray

Directions:

1. Mix the all the bell peppers, pepper, salt, and the eggs in a mixing bowl.
2. Toss well to combine.
3. Before cooking, heat your air fryer to 350 degrees F/ 175 degrees C.
4. Gently grease a baking pan that fits in your air fryer with cooking spray.
5. Pour in the egg mixture and spread it well.
6. Top the mixture with Mozzarella and cook in the preheated air fryer for 20 minutes.
7. When cooked, remove from the air fryer and serve hot on plates.
8. Enjoy your breakfast!

Egg Soufflé With Mushroom And Broccoli

Servings: 4
Cooking Time: 20 Minutes

Ingredients:

- 4 large eggs
- 1 teaspoon onion powder
- 1 teaspoon garlic powder
- 1 teaspoon red pepper, crushed
- ½ cup broccoli florets, chopped
- ½ cup mushrooms, chopped

Directions:

1. Sprinkle 4 ramekins with cooking spray and set aside.
2. In a suitable bowl, whisk eggs with onion powder, garlic powder, and red pepper.
3. Add mushrooms and broccoli and stir well.
4. Pour egg mixture into the prepared ramekins and place ramekins into the air fryer basket.
5. Cook at almost 350 degrees F/ 175 degrees C for almost 15 minutes. Make sure soufflé is cooked if soufflé is not cooked then cook for 5 minutes more.
6. Serve and enjoy.

Yogurt Eggs With Chives

Servings: 4
Cooking Time: 20 Minutes
Ingredients:
- Cooking spray
- Salt and black pepper to the taste
- 1 ½ cups Greek yogurt
- 4 eggs, whisked
- 1 tablespoon chives, chopped
- 1 tablespoon cilantro, chopped

Directions:
1. Mix the Greek yogurt, eggs, chives, salt, and black pepper in a bowl, and whisk well. Using the cooking spray, grease a suitable pan that fits the air fryer.
2. Pour in the egg mixture evenly on the pan.
3. Transfer the pan to the air fryer and cook inside at 360 degrees F/ 180 degrees C for 20 minutes. When cooked, divide the omelet and serve on plates.
4. Enjoy your breakfast!

Appetizers And Snacks Recipes

Root Veggie Chips With Herb Salt

Servings:2
Cooking Time: 8 Minutes
Ingredients:
- 1 parsnip, washed
- 1 small beet, washed
- 1 small turnip, washed
- ½ small sweet potato, washed
- 1 teaspoon olive oil
- Cooking spray
- Herb Salt:
- ¼ teaspoon kosher salt
- 2 teaspoons finely chopped fresh parsley

Directions:
1. Preheat the air fryer to 360°F (182°C).
2. Peel and thinly slice the parsnip, beet, turnip, and sweet potato, then place the vegetables in a large bowl, add the olive oil, and toss.
3. Spray the air fryer basket with cooking spray, then place the vegetables in the basket and air fry for 8 minutes, gently shaking the basket halfway through.
4. While the chips cook, make the herb salt in a small bowl by combining the kosher salt and parsley.
5. Remove the chips and place on a serving plate, then sprinkle the herb salt on top and allow to cool for 2 to 3 minutes before serving.

Enticing Pork Meatballs

Servings: 8
Cooking Time: 17 Minutes
Ingredients:
- 1 teaspoon cayenne pepper
- 2 teaspoons mustard
- 2 tablespoons Brie cheese, grated
- 5 garlic cloves, minced
- 2 small-sized yellow onions, peeled and chopped
- 1½ pounds ground pork
- Salt and black pepper, to taste

Directions:
1. Mix the cayenne pepper, mustard, grated Brie cheese, minced garlic, yellow onion, ground pork, salt, and pepper until everything is well incorporated.
2. Now, form the mixture into balls the size of golf a ball.
3. Cook for 17 minutes at 375 degrees F/ 190 degrees C.
4. Serve with your favorite sauce.

Broccoli-spinach Dip

Servings: 4
Cooking Time: 9 To 14 Minutes
Ingredients:
- ½ cup low-fat Greek yogurt
- ¼ cup nonfat cream cheese
- ½ cup frozen chopped broccoli, thawed and drained
- ½ cup frozen chopped spinach, thawed and drained
- ⅓ cup chopped red bell pepper
- 1 garlic clove, minced
- ½ teaspoon dried oregano
- 2 tablespoons grated low-sodium Parmesan cheese

Directions:
1. In a medium bowl, blend the yogurt and cream cheese until well combined.
2. Stir in the broccoli, spinach, red bell pepper, garlic, and oregano. Transfer to a 6-by-2-inch pan.
3. Sprinkle with the Parmesan cheese.
4. Place the pan in the air fryer basket. Bake for 9 to 14 minutes, until the dip is bubbly and the top starts to brown. Serve immediately.

Honey-glazed Chicken Drumettes

Servings: 6
Cooking Time: 28 Minutes

Ingredients:

- 1 ½ pounds chicken drumettes
- Salt and black pepper, to taste
- 2 tablespoons fresh chives, roughly chopped
- Teriyaki Sauce:
- 1 tablespoon sesame oil
- ¼ cup soy sauce
- ½ cup water
- ¼ cup honey
- ½ teaspoon Five-spice powder
- 2 tablespoons rice wine vinegar
- ½ teaspoon fresh ginger, grated
- 2 garlic cloves, crushed
- 1 tablespoon corn starch
- 3 tablespoons of water

Directions:

1. At 380 degrees F/ 195 degrees C, preheat your air fryer.
2. Rub the cleaned chicken drumettes with some black pepper and salt.
3. Cook in the preheated air fryer almost 15 minutes.
4. Turn them and continue cooking for 7 minutes.
5. Meanwhile, mix soy sauce, sesame oil, honey, five-spice powder, water, ginger, vinegar, and garlic in a pan over medium heat.
6. Cook for 5 minutes, with occasional stirring.
7. Add the cornstarch slurry, reduce the heat, and let it simmer until the glaze thickens.
8. After that, brush the glaze all over the chicken drumettes.
9. Air-fry for 6 minutes more.
10. Serve with the remaining glaze on top and garnished with fresh chives.
11. Serve

Crispy Mustard Fried Leek

Servings: 4
Cooking Time: 10 Minutes
Ingredients:
- 1 large-sized leek, cut into ½-inch wide rings
- Black pepper and salt, to taste
- 1 teaspoon mustard
- 1 cup milk
- 1 egg
- ½ cup almond flour
- ½ teaspoon baking powder
- ½ cup pork rinds, crushed

Directions:
1. Toss your leeks with black pepper and salt.
2. In a suitable mixing bowl, whisk the mustard, milk and egg until frothy and pale.
3. Now, combine almond flour and baking powder in another mixing bowl. In the third bowl, place the pork rinds.
4. Coat the leek slices with the almond meal mixture.
5. Dredge the floured leek slices into the milk/egg mixture, coating well. Finally, roll them over the pork rinds.
6. Air-fry for approximately 10 minutes at 370 degrees F/ 185 degrees C. Serve!

Roasted Almonds With Paprika

Servings: 8
Cooking Time: 8 Minutes
Ingredients:
- 2 cups almonds
- ¼ teaspoon black pepper
- 1 teaspoon paprika
- 1 tablespoon garlic powder
- 1 tablespoon soy sauce

Directions:
1. Add black pepper, paprika, garlic powder, and soy sauce in a suitable bowl and stir well.
2. Add almonds and stir to coat.
3. Grease its air fryer basket with cooking spray.
4. Add almonds in air fryer basket and cook for 6-8 minutes at 320 degrees F/ 160 degrees C.
5. Serve and enjoy.

Apple Chips

Servings: 4
Cooking Time: 10 Minutes

Ingredients:
- 4 medium apples (any type will work), cored
- ¼ teaspoon cinnamon
- ¼ teaspoon nutmeg

Directions:
1. Cut the apples into ⅓-inch-thick slices. Thin slices yield crunchy chips.
2. Place the apple slices in a large bowl. Sprinkle the cinnamon and nutmeg onto the apple slices.
3. Transfer the apple chips to the air fryer. It is okay to stack them. Cook for 6 minutes.
4. Open the air fryer and shake the basket. Cook for an additional 4 minutes, or until crunchy.
5. Cool before serving.

Spicy Chickpeas

Servings: 4
Cooking Time: 20 Minutes

Ingredients:
- Olive oil
- ½ teaspoon ground cumin
- ½ teaspoon chili powder
- ¼ teaspoon cayenne pepper
- ¼ teaspoon salt
- 1 (19-ounce) can chickpeas, drained and rinsed

Directions:
1. Spray a fryer basket lightly with olive oil.
2. In a small bowl, combine the cumin, chili powder, cayenne pepper, and salt.
3. In a medium bowl, add the chickpeas and lightly spray them with olive oil. Add the spice mixture and toss until coated evenly.
4. Transfer the chickpeas to the fryer basket. Air fry until the chickpeas reach your desired level of crunchiness, 15 to 20 minutes, making sure to shake the basket every 5 minutes.

Delectable Chaffles

Servings: 4
Cooking Time: 25 Minutes
Ingredients:
- 4 eggs, beaten
- 2 oz. bacon, chopped, cooked
- 1 cucumber, pickled, grated
- 2 oz. Cheddar cheese, shredded
- ¼ teaspoon salt
- ½ teaspoon ground black pepper
- Cooking spray

Directions:
1. The chaffle batter should be cooked.
2. Spray the air fryer pan with cooking spray.
3. Mix up eggs, bacon, pickled cucumber, cheese, salt, and ground black pepper in a mixing bowl. Whisk the mixture gently.
4. Pour ¼ part of the liquid on the pan.
5. Arrange the pan to the air fryer and cook the chaffle for 6 minutes at 400 degrees F/ 205 degrees C.
6. When cooked, transfer the cooked chaffle in the plate.
7. Repeat the same steps with the remaining chaffle batter and you should get 4 chaffles.
8. Enjoy.

Cajun Zucchini Chips

Servings: 4
Cooking Time: 15 Minutes
Ingredients:
- Olive oil
- 2 large zucchini, cut into ⅛-inch-thick slices
- 2 teaspoons Cajun seasoning

Directions:
1. Spray a fryer basket lightly with olive oil.
2. Put the zucchini slices in a medium bowl and spray them generously with olive oil.
3. Sprinkle the Cajun seasoning over the zucchini and stir to make sure they are evenly coated with oil and seasoning.
4. Place slices in a single layer in the fryer basket, making sure not to overcrowd. You will need to cook these in several batches.
5. Air fry for 8 minutes. Flip the slices over and air fry until they are as crisp and brown as you prefer, an additional 7 to 8 minutes.

Fried Bacon Slices

Servings: 11
Cooking Time: 10 Minutes
Ingredients:

- 11 bacon slices

Directions:

1. Place ½ bacon slices in air fryer basket.
2. Cook at almost 400 degrees F/ 205 degrees C for almost 10 minutes.
3. Cook remaining ½ bacon slices using same steps.
4. Serve and enjoy.

Artichoke-spinach Dip

Servings:3
Cooking Time: 10 Minutes
Ingredients:

- 1 (14-ounce / 397-g) can artichoke hearts packed in water, drained and chopped
- 1 (10-ounce / 284-g) package frozen spinach, thawed and drained
- 1 teaspoon minced garlic
- 2 tablespoons mayonnaise
- ¼ cup nonfat plain Greek yogurt
- ¼ cup shredded part-skim Mozzarella cheese
- ¼ cup grated Parmesan cheese
- ¼ teaspoon freshly ground black pepper
- Cooking spray

Directions:

1. Preheat the air fryer to 360°F (182°C).
2. Wrap the artichoke hearts and spinach in a paper towel and squeeze out any excess liquid, then transfer the vegetables to a large bowl.
3. Add the minced garlic, mayonnaise, plain Greek yogurt, Mozzarella, Parmesan, and black pepper to the large bowl, stirring well to combine.
4. Spray a baking pan with cooking spray, then transfer the dip mixture to the pan and air fry for 10 minutes.
5. Remove the dip from the air fryer and allow to cool in the pan on a wire rack for 10 minutes before serving.

Air Fried Shrimp & Bacon

Servings: 4-6
Cooking Time: 10 Minutes

Ingredients:
- 16 ounces sliced bacon
- 20 ounces peeled shrimp, deveined

Directions:
1. Prepare your clean air fryer.
2. Preheat the air fryer for 4 to 5 minutes at 390 degrees F/ 200 degrees C.
3. Make the shrimps under the bacon regularly. Put them in the refrigerator and cool for 15 to 20 minutes.
4. After that, take out the shrimps and place them in the air-frying basket.
5. Let the shrimps be cooked for 6 minutes in the air fryer.
6. Serve and enjoy!

Roasted Buttery Cashews

Servings: 8
Cooking Time: 4 Minutes

Ingredients:
- 2 cups raw cashew nuts
- 1 teaspoon butter, melted
- Salt and freshly black pepper, as needed

Directions:
1. At 355 degrees F/ 180 degrees C, preheat your air fryer.
2. In a suitable bowl, mix together all the recipe ingredients.
3. Place the cashews nuts in an air fryer basket in a single layer. You can lay a piece of grease-proof baking paper.
4. Air fry for about 4 minutes, shaking once halfway through.
5. Serve.

Corn With Coriander And Parmesan Cheese

Servings: 2
Cooking Time: 15 Minutes

Ingredients:

- 2 ears corn, husked and cleaned
- 1 tablespoon melted butter
- 1 tablespoon fresh coriander, finely chopped
- 2 tablespoons Parmesan cheese, finely chopped

Directions:

1. Butter the corn and then arrange the corn in the air fryer.
2. Cook for 14 minutes at 400 degrees F/ 205 degrees C.
3. When done, serve warm and top with the Parmesan cheese and fresh coriander.
4. Bon appétit!

Buffalo Breaded Cauliflower Bites

Servings: 4
Cooking Time: 25 Minutes

Ingredients:

- 1 cup all-purpose flour
- 1 cup water
- 1 teaspoon garlic powder
- 1 large head cauliflower, cut into florets (4 cups)
- Cooking oil
- ⅓ cup Frank's RedHot Buffalo Wings sauce

Directions:

1. In a large bowl, combine the flour, water, and garlic powder. Mix well. The mixture should resemble pancake batter.
2. Add the cauliflower to the batter and stir to coat. Transfer the cauliflower to another large bowl to drain the excess batter.
3. Spray the air fryer with cooking oil.
4. Transfer the cauliflower to the air fryer. Do not stack. Cook in batches. Spray the cauliflower with cooking oil. Cook for 6 minutes.
5. Open the air fryer and transfer the cauliflower to a large bowl. Drizzle with the Buffalo sauce. Mix well.
6. Return the cauliflower to the air fryer. Cook for an additional 6 minutes, or until crisp.
7. Remove the cooked cauliflower from the air fryer, then repeat steps 4 through 6 for the remaining cauliflower batches.
8. Cool before serving.

Crispy Old Bay Chicken Wings

Servings: 4
Cooking Time: 15 Minutes
Ingredients:
- Olive oil
- 2 tablespoons Old Bay seasoning
- 2 teaspoons baking powder
- 2 teaspoons salt
- 2 pounds chicken wings

Directions:
1. Spray a fryer basket lightly with olive oil.
2. In a large zip-top plastic bag, mix together the Old Bay seasoning, baking powder, and salt.
3. Pat the wings dry with paper towels.
4. Place the wings in the zip-top bag, seal, and toss with the seasoning mixture until evenly coated.
5. Place the seasoned wings in the fryer basket in a single layer. Lightly spray with olive oil. You may need to cook them in batches.
6. Air fry for 7 minutes. Turn the wings over, lightly spray them with olive oil, and air fry until the wings are crispy and lightly browned, 5 to 8 more minutes. Using a meat thermometer, check to make sure the internal temperature is 165°F or higher.

Breaded Artichoke Hearts

Servings: 14
Cooking Time: 8 Minutes
Ingredients:
- 14 whole artichoke hearts, packed in water
- 1 egg
- ½ cup all-purpose flour
- ⅓ cup panko bread crumbs
- 1 teaspoon Italian seasoning
- Cooking spray

Directions:
1. Preheat the air fryer to 380°F (193°C)
2. Squeeze excess water from the artichoke hearts and place them on paper towels to dry.
3. In a small bowl, beat the egg. In another small bowl, place the flour. In a third small bowl, combine the bread crumbs and Italian seasoning, and stir.
4. Spritz the air fryer basket with cooking spray.
5. Dip the artichoke hearts in the flour, then the egg, and then the bread crumb mixture.
6. Place the breaded artichoke hearts in the air fryer. Spray them with cooking spray. Air fry for 8 minutes, or until the artichoke hearts have browned and are crisp, flipping once halfway through.
7. Let cool for 5 minutes before serving.

Peppery Chicken Meatballs

Servings: 16
Cooking Time: 13 To 20 Minutes

Ingredients:

- 2 teaspoons olive oil
- ¼ cup minced onion
- ¼ cup minced red bell pepper
- 2 vanilla wafers, crushed
- 1 egg white
- ½ teaspoon dried thyme
- ½ pound (227 g) ground chicken breast

Directions:

1. Preheat the air fryer to 370°F (188°C).
2. In a baking pan, mix the olive oil, onion, and red bell pepper. Put the pan in the air fryer. Air fry for 3 to 5 minutes, or until the vegetables are tender.
3. In a medium bowl, mix the cooked vegetables, crushed wafers, egg white, and thyme until well combined
4. Mix in the chicken, gently but thoroughly, until everything is combined.
5. Form the mixture into 16 meatballs and place them in the air fryer basket. Air fry for 10 to 15 minutes, or until the meatballs reach an internal temperature of 165°F (74°C) on a meat thermometer.
6. Serve immediately.

Spinach And Artichoke Dip Wontons

Servings: 20
Cooking Time: 40 Minutes

Ingredients:

- 6 ounces cream cheese
- ¼ cup sour cream
- ¼ cup shredded Parmesan cheese
- ¼ cup shredded mozzarella cheese
- 5 ounces frozen chopped spinach, thawed and drained
- 6 ounces marinated artichoke hearts, drained
- 2 garlic cloves, chopped
- Salt
- Pepper
- 20 wonton wrappers
- Cooking oil

Directions:

1. In a small, microwave-safe bowl, heat the cream cheese in the microwave for 20 seconds to soften.
2. In a medium bowl, combine the cream cheese, sour cream, Parmesan, mozzarella, spinach, artichoke hearts, garlic, and salt and pepper to taste. Stir to mix well.
3. Lay out the wonton wrappers on a work surface. A clean table or large cutting board works well.
4. Scoop 1½ teaspoons of the artichoke mixture onto each wrapper. Be careful not to overfill.
5. Fold each wrapper diagonally to form a triangle. Bring the two bottom corners up toward each other. Do not close the wrapper yet. Bring up the two open sides and push out any air. Squeeze the open edges together to seal.
6. Place the wontons in the air fryer basket and cook in batches, or stack (see Air fryer cooking tip). Spray the wontons with cooking oil. Cook for 10 minutes.
7. Remove the basket and flip the wontons. Return to the air fryer and cook for an additional 5 to 8 minutes, until the wontons have reached your desired level of golden-brown crispiness.
8. If cooking in batches, remove the cooked wontons from the air fryer, then repeat steps 6 and 7 for the remaining wontons.
9. Cool before serving.

Salmon Nachos

Servings: 6
Cooking Time: 9 To 12 Minutes
Ingredients:
- 2 ounces (about 36) baked no-salt corn tortilla chips (see Tip)
- 1 (5-ounce) baked salmon fillet, flaked
- ½ cup canned low-sodium black beans, rinsed and drained
- 1 red bell pepper, chopped
- ½ cup grated carrot
- 1 jalapeño pepper, minced
- ⅓ cup shredded low-sodium low-fat Swiss cheese
- 1 tomato, chopped

Directions:
1. In a 6-by-2-inch pan, layer the tortilla chips. Top with the salmon, black beans, red bell pepper, carrot, jalapeño, and Swiss cheese.
2. Bake in the air fryer for 9 to 12 minutes, or until the cheese is melted and starts to brown.
3. Top with the tomato and serve.

Cheese Sticks With Coconut

Servings: 4
Cooking Time: 4 Minutes
Ingredients:
- 1 egg, beaten
- 4 tablespoons coconut flakes
- 1 teaspoon ground paprika
- 6 oz. Provolone cheese
- Cooking spray

Directions:
1. Cut the cheese into sticks.
2. Dip every cheese stick in the beaten egg.
3. After this, mix up coconut flakes and ground paprika.
4. Coat the cheese sticks in the coconut mixture.
5. Preheat the air fryer to degrees F/ 205 degrees C. Put the cheese sticks in the air fryer and spray them with cooking spray.
6. Cook the meal for 2 minutes from each side.
7. Cool them well before serving.

Poultry Recipes
Parmesan Chicken Wings

Servings: 4
Cooking Time: 16 To 18 Minutes

Ingredients:

- 1¼ cups grated Parmesan cheese
- 1 tablespoon garlic powder
- 1 teaspoon salt
- ½ teaspoon freshly ground black pepper
- ¾ cup all-purpose flour
- 1 large egg, beaten
- 12 chicken wings (about 1 pound / 454 g)
- Cooking spray

Directions:

1. Preheat the air fryer to 390°F (199°C). Line the air fryer basket with parchment paper.
2. In a shallow bowl, whisk the Parmesan cheese, garlic powder, salt, and pepper until blended. Place the flour in a second shallow bowl and the beaten egg in a third shallow bowl.
3. One at a time, dip the chicken wings into the flour, the beaten egg, and the Parmesan cheese mixture, coating thoroughly.
4. Place the chicken wings on the parchment and spritz with cooking spray.
5. Air fry for 8 minutes. Flip the chicken, spritz it with cooking spray, and air fry for 8 to 10 minutes more until the internal temperature reaches 165°F (74°C) and the insides are no longer pink. Let sit for 5 minutes before serving.

Spicy Asian Chicken Thighs With Soy Sauce

Servings: 4
Cooking Time: 20 Minutes

Ingredients:

- 4 chicken thighs, skin-on, and bone-in
- 2 teaspoons ginger, grated
- 1 lime juice
- 2 tablespoons chili garlic sauce
- ¼ cup olive oil
- ⅓ cup soy sauce

Directions:

1. In a suitable bowl, whisk together chili garlic sauce, ginger, lime juice, soy sauce oil.
2. Add chicken to the same bowl and coat well with the prepared marinade, cover and place in the refrigerator for almost 30 minutes.
3. Set marinated chicken in your air fryer basket and air fryer at 400 degrees F/ 205 degrees C for 15-20 minutes.
4. Serve and enjoy.

Marjoram Chicken Drumsticks

Servings: 3
Cooking Time: 30 Minutes

Ingredients:

- 3 chicken drumsticks
- Sea salt, to taste
- Ground black pepper, to season
- ½ teaspoon red pepper flakes, crushed
- ½ teaspoon shallot powder
- ½ teaspoon onion powder
- ½ teaspoon garlic powder
- 1 teaspoon dried marjoram
- ¼ cup cornstarch
- 2 tablespoons balsamic vinegar
- 2 tablespoons milk

Directions:

1. Before cooking, heat your air fryer to 380 degrees F/ 195 degrees C.
2. Using the paper towels, pat the chicken dry. To season, rub the chicken drumsticks with all seasonings.
3. Mix balsamic vinegar, milk, and cornstarch together in a shallow bowl.
4. Dredge the chicken drumsticks in the cornstarch mixture and press the drumsticks to coat thoroughly. Then shake off any excess mixture.
5. Set the temperature to 380 degrees F/ 195 degrees C and timer for 30 minutes.
6. Halfway through cooking, flip the chicken.
7. Serve and enjoy!

Spice Chicken Pieces

Servings: 6
Cooking Time: 20 Minutes

Ingredients:

- 3 pounds' chicken, cut into eight pieces
- ¼ teaspoon cayenne
- 1 teaspoon paprika
- 2 teaspoons onion powder
- 1 ½ teaspoons garlic powder
- 1 ½ teaspoons dried oregano
- ½ tablespoon dried thyme
- Black pepper
- Salt

Directions:

1. Season chicken with black pepper and salt.
2. In a suitable bowl, mix together spices and herbs and rub spice mixture over chicken pieces.
3. Spray its air fryer basket with cooking spray.
4. Place prepared chicken in air fryer basket and cook at 350 degrees F/ 175 degrees C for almost 20 minutes, turning halfway through.
5. Serve and enjoy.

Honey Turkey Tenderloin

Servings: 4
Cooking Time: 55 Minutes
Ingredients:

- 1 tablespoon honey
- ¼ cup vermouth
- 2 tablespoons lemon juice
- 1 teaspoon marjoram
- 1 teaspoon oregano, dried
- 1 turkey tenderloin, quartered
- 1 tablespoon sesame oil
- Sea salt flakes as needed
- ¾ teaspoon smoked paprika
- 1 teaspoon crushed sage leaves, dried
- ½ teaspoon ground pepper

Directions:
1. To marinate, combine honey, vermouth, lemon juice, marjoram, and oregano together in a zip-lock bag.
2. Seal and marinate at room temperature for 3 hours.
3. On a flat kitchen surface, plug your air fryer and turn it on.
4. Before cooking, heat your air fryer to 355 degrees F/ 180 degrees C for 4 to 5 minutes.
5. Gently coat the air fryer basket with cooking oil or spray.
6. Place the turkey tenderloin inside the air fryer basket.
7. Cook in your air fryer for 50 to 55 minutes.
8. When cooked, remove from the air fryer and serve warm.

Lemon Parmesan Chicken

Servings: 4
Cooking Time: 20 Minutes
Ingredients:

- 1 egg
- 2 tablespoons lemon juice
- 2 teaspoons minced garlic
- ½ teaspoon salt
- ½ teaspoon freshly ground black pepper
- 4 boneless, skinless chicken breasts, thin cut
- Olive oil spray
- ½ cup whole-wheat bread crumbs
- ¼ cup grated Parmesan cheese

Directions:
1. In a medium bowl, whisk together the egg, lemon juice, garlic, salt, and pepper. Add the chicken breasts, cover, and refrigerate for up to 1 hour.
2. In a shallow bowl, combine the bread crumbs and Parmesan cheese.
3. Preheat the air fryer to 360°F (182°C). Spray the air fryer basket lightly with olive oil spray.
4. Remove the chicken breasts from the egg mixture, then dredge them in the bread crumb mixture, and place in the air fryer basket in a single layer. Lightly spray the chicken breasts with olive oil spray. You may need to cook the chicken in batches.
5. Air fry for 8 minutes. Flip the chicken over, lightly spray with olive oil spray, and air fry until the chicken reaches an internal temperature of 165°F (74°C), for an additional 7 to 12 minutes.
6. Serve warm.

Cheesy Chicken Tacos

Servings: 4
Cooking Time: 12 To 16 Minutes

Ingredients:

- 1 teaspoon chili powder
- ½ teaspoon ground cumin
- ½ teaspoon garlic powder
- Salt and pepper, to taste
- Pinch cayenne pepper
- 1 pound (454 g) boneless, skinless chicken thighs, trimmed
- 1 teaspoon vegetable oil
- 1 tomato, cored and chopped
- 2 tablespoons finely chopped red onion
- 2 teaspoons minced jalapeño chile
- 1½ teaspoons lime juice
- 6 to 12 (6-inch) corn tortillas, warmed
- 1 cup shredded iceberg lettuce
- 3 ounces (85 g) cheddar cheese, shredded (¾ cup)

Directions:

1. Preheat the air fryer to 400°F (204°C).
2. Combine chili powder, cumin, garlic powder, ½ teaspoon salt, ¼ teaspoon pepper, and cayenne in bowl. Pat chicken dry with paper towels, rub with oil, and sprinkle evenly with spice mixture. Place chicken in air fryer basket. Air fry until chicken registers 165°F (74°C), 12 to 16 minutes, flipping chicken halfway through cooking.
3. Meanwhile, combine tomato, onion, jalapeño, and lime juice in a bowl; season with salt and pepper to taste and set aside until ready to serve.
4. Transfer chicken to a cutting board, let cool slightly, then shred into bite-size pieces using 2 forks. Serve chicken on warm tortillas, topped with salsa, lettuce, and cheddar.

Chicken & Mushroom Meatballs

Servings: 2
Cooking Time: 18 Minutes

Ingredients:

- ½ pound boneless chicken thighs
- 1 teaspoon minced garlic
- 1-¼ cup roasted pecans
- ½ cup mushrooms
- 1 teaspoon extra virgin olive oil

Directions:

1. At 375 degrees F/ 190 degrees C, preheat your Air fryer.
2. Cube the chicken thighs.
3. Place them in the food processor along with the garlic, pecans, and other seasonings as desired. Pulse until a smooth consistency is achieved.
4. Chop the mushrooms finely, then add them to the chicken mixture and combine well.
5. Shape the mixture into balls with your hands and brush them with olive oil.
6. Put the balls into the air fryer and cook for 18 minutes.
7. Serve hot.

Italian Chicken And Veggies

Servings: 4
Cooking Time: 30 Minutes

Ingredients:
- ¾ cup balsamic vinaigrette dressing, divided
- 1 pound boneless, skinless chicken tenderloins
- Olive oil
- 1 pound fresh green beans, trimmed
- 1 pint grape tomatoes

Directions:
1. Place ½ cup of the balsamic vinaigrette dressing and the chicken in a large zip-top plastic bag, seal, and refrigerate for at least 1 hour or up to overnight.
2. In a large bowl, mix together the green beans, tomatoes, and the remaining ¼ cup of balsamic vinaigrette dressing until well coated.
3. Spray the fryer basket lightly with oil. Place the vegetables in the fryer basket. Reserve any remaining vinaigrette.
4. Air fry for 8 minutes. Shake the basket and continue to cook until the beans are crisp but tender, and the tomatoes are soft and slightly charred, an additional 5 to 7 minutes.
5. Wipe the fryer basket with a paper towel and spray lightly with olive oil.
6. Place the chicken in the fryer basket in a single layer. You may need to cook them in batches.
7. Air fry for 7 minutes. Flip the chicken over, baste with some of the remaining vinaigrette, and cook until the chicken reaches an internal temperature of 165°F, an additional 5 to 8 minutes.
8. Serve the chicken and veggies together.

Potato Cheese Crusted Chicken

Servings: 4
Cooking Time: 22 To 25 Minutes

Ingredients:
- ¼ cup buttermilk
- 1 large egg, beaten
- 1 cup instant potato flakes
- ¼ cup grated Parmesan cheese
- 1 teaspoon salt
- ½ teaspoon freshly ground black pepper
- 2 whole boneless, skinless chicken breasts (about 1 pound / 454 g each), halved
- Cooking spray

Directions:
1. Preheat the air fryer to 325°F (163°C). Line the air fryer basket with parchment paper.
2. In a shallow bowl, whisk the buttermilk and egg until blended. In another shallow bowl, stir together the potato flakes, cheese, salt, and pepper.
3. One at a time, dip the chicken pieces in the buttermilk mixture and the potato flake mixture, coating thoroughly.
4. Place the coated chicken on the parchment and spritz with cooking spray.
5. Bake for 15 minutes. Flip the chicken, spritz it with cooking spray, and bake for 7 to 10 minutes more until the outside is crispy and the inside is no longer pink. Serve immediately.

Chicken And Vegetable Fajitas

Servings: 6
Cooking Time: 23 Minutes

Ingredients:
- Chicken:
- 1 pound (454 g) boneless, skinless chicken thighs, cut crosswise into thirds
- 1 tablespoon vegetable oil
- 4½ teaspoons taco seasoning
- Vegetables
- 1 cup sliced onion
- 1 cup sliced bell pepper
- 1 or 2 jalapeños, quartered lengthwise
- 1 tablespoon vegetable oil
- ½ teaspoon kosher salt
- ½ teaspoon ground cumin
- For Serving:
- Tortillas
- Sour cream
- Shredded cheese
- Guacamole
- Salsa

Directions:
1. Preheat the air fryer to 375°F (191°C).
2. For the chicken: In a medium bowl, toss together the chicken, vegetable oil, and taco seasoning to coat.
3. For the vegetables: In a separate bowl, toss together the onion, bell pepper, jalapeño (s), vegetable oil, salt, and cumin to coat.
4. Place the chicken in the air fryer basket. Air fry for 10 minutes. Add the vegetables to the basket, toss everything together to blend the seasonings, and air fry for 13 minutes more. Use a meat thermometer to ensure the chicken has reached an internal temperature of 165°F (74°C).
5. Transfer the chicken and vegetables to a serving platter. Serve with tortillas and the desired fajita fixings.

Breaded Homestyle Chicken Strips

Servings: 4
Cooking Time: 20 Minutes

Ingredients:

- 1 tablespoon of olive oil, plus more for spraying
- 1 pound boneless, skinless chicken tenderloins
- 1 teaspoon salt
- ½ teaspoon freshly ground black pepper
- ½ teaspoon paprika
- ½ teaspoon garlic powder
- ½ cup whole-wheat seasoned bread crumbs
- 1 teaspoon dried parsley

Directions:

1. Spray a fryer basket lightly with olive oil.
2. In a medium bowl, toss the chicken with the salt, pepper, paprika, and garlic powder until evenly coated.
3. Add the olive oil and toss to coat the chicken evenly.
4. In a separate, shallow bowl, mix together the bread crumbs and parsley.
5. Coat each piece of chicken evenly in the bread crumb mixture.
6. Place the chicken in the fryer basket in a single layer and spray it lightly with olive oil. You may need to cook them in batches.
7. Air fry for 10 minutes. Flip the chicken over, lightly spray with olive oil, and cook until golden brown, an additional 8 to 10 minutes.

Spice Chicken Wings With Parmesan Cheese

Servings: 3
Cooking Time: 22 Minutes

Ingredients:

- ¼ cup almond meal
- ¼ cup flaxseed meal
- 2 tablespoons butter, melted
- 6 tablespoons Parmesan cheese, preferably freshly grated
- 1 tablespoon Ranch seasoning mix
- 2 tablespoons oyster sauce
- 6 chicken wings, bone-in

Directions:

1. At 370 degrees F/ 185 degrees C, preheat your Air Fryer.
2. In a re-sealable bag, place the almond meal, flaxseed meal, butter, parmesan, Ranch seasoning mix, and oyster sauce.
3. Add the chicken wings in the sealed bag and shake to coat on all sides.
4. Arrange the chicken wings in the air fryer basket.
5. Spritz the chicken wings with a nonstick cooking spray.
6. Cook for 11 minutes. Turn them over and cook an additional 11 minutes.
7. Serve warm.

Tasty Chicken Fajitas

Servings: 3
Cooking Time: 22 Minutes

Ingredients:
- 1 pound chicken breast, skinless and boneless
- 1 teaspoon butter, melted
- Sea salt, to taste
- Ground black pepper, to taste
- ½ teaspoon red pepper flakes, crushed
- ½ teaspoon Mexican oregano
- ½ teaspoon garlic powder
- 3 bell peppers, thinly sliced
- 1 red onion, sliced

Directions:
1. Before cooking, heat your air fryer to 380 degrees F/ 195 degrees C.
2. Using the melted butter, brush all sides of the chicken.
3. To season, rub black pepper, salt, oregano, garlic powder, and red pepper.
4. Set the cooking temperature to 380 degrees F/ 195 degrees C and timer for 12 minutes. Cook the seasoned chicken breast in your air fryer until golden brown. Flip halfway through cooking.
5. Set the chicken aside to cool for 10 minutes. Then slice into strips and reserve to keep it warm.
6. In the air fryer basket, add peppers and onions. Cook in your air fryer at 400 degrees F/ 205 degrees C for 10 minutes. Taste to adjust the seasonings and add some seasoning as you like.
7. When cooked, place the vegetables on a bowl. Stir to combine well and serve immediately!

Tex-mex Turkey Burgers

Servings: 4
Cooking Time: 14 To 16 Minutes

Ingredients:
- ⅓ cup finely crushed corn tortilla chips
- 1 egg, beaten
- ¼ cup salsa
- ⅓ cup shredded pepper Jack cheese
- Pinch salt
- Freshly ground black pepper, to taste
- 1 pound (454 g) ground turkey
- 1 tablespoon olive oil
- 1 teaspoon paprika

Directions:
1. Preheat the air fryer to 330°F (166°C).
2. In a medium bowl, combine the tortilla chips, egg, salsa, cheese, salt, and pepper, and mix well.
3. Add the turkey and mix gently but thoroughly with clean hands.
4. Form the meat mixture into patties about ½ inch thick. Make an indentation in the center of each patty with your thumb so the burgers don't puff up while cooking.
5. Brush the patties on both sides with the olive oil and sprinkle with paprika.
6. Put in the air fryer basket and air fry for 14 to 16 minutes or until the meat registers at least 165°F (74°C).
7. Let sit for 5 minutes before serving.

Creamy Chicken Breasts With Jalapeno

Servings: 2
Cooking Time: 25 Minutes
Ingredients:

- 2 ounces. full-fat cream cheese, softened
- 4 slices sugar-free bacon, cooked and crumbled
- ¼ cup pickled jalapenos, sliced
- ½ cup sharp cheddar cheese, shredded and divided
- 2 (6-ounce) boneless skinless chicken breasts

Directions:
1. Mix bacon, half of the Cheddar cheese, cream cheese, and jalapeno slices together in a mixing dish until well incorporated.
2. Cut a ¾-length slits in the chicken breasts. Be care not to cut all the way down. Six to eight slices will be made in this way, depending on the chicken breast.
3. Fill the slits with the cheese mixture divided into even sized dollops.
4. Sprinkle the remaining cheddar cheese on the top.
5. Place the chicken slices in the air fryer basket.
6. Cook in your air fryer at 350 degrees F/ 175 degrees C for 20 minutes or until the internal temperature measures 165 degrees F/ 75 degrees C.
7. When cooked, remove from the air fryer and serve hot.
8. Enjoy now!

Awesome Duck With Potato Rösti

Servings: 2
Cooking Time: 15 Minutes
Ingredients:

- ½ pound duck breast, skin-on, boneless
- 1 clove garlic, halved
- Coarse sea salt, to taste
- Ground black pepper, to taste
- ½ teaspoon marjoram
- ¼ teaspoon mustard seeds
- ¼ teaspoon fennel seeds

- Potato Rösti:
- ½ pound potatoes, grated
- 2 tablespoons butter, melted
- 1 teaspoon fresh rosemary, chopped
- Coarse sea salt, to taste
- Ground black pepper, to taste

Directions:
1. Butterfly the duck breast to render the fat: and season with fresh garlic on all sides.
2. To season, add salt, marjoram, mustard seeds, fennel seeds, and pepper.
3. Transfer the duck breast onto the air fryer basket skin-side up. Cook the duck breast in your air fryer at 400 degrees F/ 205 degrees C for 10 minutes. Flip the duck breast halfway through cooking.
4. When cooked, rest for 5 to 8 minutes before serving.
5. To make the potato rösti, mix all the ingredients in a bowl until well combined. Then make 2 equal patties from the mixture.
6. Cook the potato rösti at 400 degrees F/ 205 degrees C for 15 minutes.
7. When cooked, remove from the air fryer and serve the warm duck breast with potato rösti.

Easy Tandoori Chicken

Servings: 4
Cooking Time: 18 To 23 Minutes

Ingredients:
- ⅔ cup plain low-fat yogurt
- 2 tablespoons freshly squeezed lemon juice
- 2 teaspoons curry powder
- ½ teaspoon ground cinnamon
- 2 garlic cloves, minced
- 2 teaspoons olive oil
- 4 (5-ounce / 142-g) low-sodium boneless, skinless chicken breasts

Directions:
1. In a medium bowl, whisk the yogurt, lemon juice, curry powder, cinnamon, garlic, and olive oil.
2. With a sharp knife, cut thin slashes into the chicken. Add it to the yogurt mixture and turn to coat. Let stand for 10 minutes at room temperature. You can also prepare this ahead of time and marinate the chicken in the refrigerator for up to 24 hours.
3. Preheat the air fryer to 360°F (182°C).
4. Remove the chicken from the marinade and shake off any excess liquid. Discard any remaining marinade.
5. Roast the chicken for 10 minutes. With tongs, carefully turn each piece. Roast for 8 to 13 minutes more, or until the chicken reaches an internal temperature of 165°F (74°C) on a meat thermometer. Serve immediately.

Spice Chicken With Broccoli

Servings: 4
Cooking Time: 20 Minutes

Ingredients:
- 1-pound chicken breast, boneless, and cut into chunks
- 2 cups broccoli florets
- 2 teaspoons hot sauce
- 2 teaspoons vinegar
- 1 teaspoon sesame oil
- 1 tablespoon soy sauce
- 1 tablespoon ginger, minced
- ½ teaspoon garlic powder
- 1 tablespoon olive oil
- ½ onion, sliced
- Black pepper
- Salt

Directions:
1. Add all the recipe ingredients into the suitable mixing bowl and toss well.
2. Grease its air fryer basket with cooking spray.
3. Transfer chicken and broccoli mixture into the air fryer basket.
4. Cook at almost 380 degrees F/ 195 degrees C for almost 15-20 minutes. Shake halfway through.
5. Serve and enjoy.

Roasted Chicken And Vegetable Salad

Servings: 4
Cooking Time: 10 To 13 Minutes

Ingredients:
- 3 (4-ounce / 113-g) low-sodium boneless, skinless chicken breasts, cut into 1-inch cubes
- 1 small red onion, sliced
- 1 red bell pepper, sliced
- 1 cup green beans, cut into 1-inch pieces
- 2 tablespoons low-fat ranch salad dressing
- 2 tablespoons freshly squeezed lemon juice
- ½ teaspoon dried basil
- 4 cups mixed lettuce

Directions:
1. Preheat the air fryer to 400°F (204°C).
2. In the air fryer basket, roast the chicken, red onion, red bell pepper, and green beans for 10 to 13 minutes, or until the chicken reaches an internal temperature of 165°F (74°C) on a meat thermometer, tossing the food in the basket once during cooking.
3. While the chicken cooks, in a serving bowl, mix the ranch dressing, lemon juice, and basil.
4. Transfer the chicken and vegetables to a serving bowl and toss with the dressing to coat. Serve immediately on lettuce leaves.

Crispy Chicken Cordon Bleu

Servings: 4
Cooking Time: 13 To 15 Minutes

Ingredients:
- 4 chicken breast fillets
- ¼ cup chopped ham
- ⅓ cup grated Swiss or Gruyère cheese
- ¼ cup flour
- Pinch salt
- Freshly ground black pepper, to taste
- ½ teaspoon dried marjoram
- 1 egg
- 1 cup panko bread crumbs
- Olive oil for misting

Directions:
1. Preheat the air fryer to 380°F (193°C).
2. Put the chicken breast fillets on a work surface and gently press them with the palm of your hand to make them a bit thinner. Don't tear the meat.
3. In a small bowl, combine the ham and cheese. Divide this mixture among the chicken fillets. Wrap the chicken around the filling to enclose it, using toothpicks to hold the chicken together.
4. In a shallow bowl, mix the flour, salt, pepper, and marjoram. In another bowl, beat the egg. Spread the bread crumbs out on a plate.
5. Dip the chicken into the flour mixture, then into the egg, then into the bread crumbs to coat thoroughly.
6. Put the chicken in the air fryer basket and mist with olive oil.
7. Bake for 13 to 15 minutes or until the chicken is thoroughly cooked to 165°F (74°C). Carefully remove the toothpicks and serve.

Crispy Chicken And Pickles Sandwich

Servings: 4
Cooking Time: 25 Minutes

Ingredients:

- 2 (4-ounce) boneless, skinless chicken breasts
- 1 cup dill pickle juice
- 1 cup milk, divided
- Cooking oil
- 1 egg
- ½ cup all-purpose flour
- Salt
- Pepper
- 4 buns
- Pickles

Directions:

1. With your knife blade parallel to the cutting board, slice the chicken breasts in half horizontally to create 4 thin cutlets.
2. Place the chicken in a large bowl. Add the pickle juice and ½ cup of milk, and toss to coat.
3. Allow the chicken to marinate in the refrigerator for at least 30 minutes.
4. Spray the air fryer pan with cooking oil.
5. In a bowl large enough to dip a chicken cutlet, beat the egg and add the remaining ½ cup of milk. Stir to combine. In another bowl, place the flour and season with salt and pepper.
6. When done marinating, dip each chicken cutlet in the egg and milk mixture and then the flour.
7. Place 2 chicken cutlets in the air fryer. Spray them with cooking oil. Cook for 6 minutes.
8. Open the air fryer and flip the chicken. Cook for an additional 6 minutes.
9. Remove the cooked chicken from the air fryer, then repeat steps 7 and 8 for the remaining 2 chicken cutlets.
10. Serve on buns with pickles.

Beef, Pork & Lamb Recipes
Authentic Greek Vegetable Skillet

Servings: 4
Cooking Time: 20 Minutes
Ingredients:
- ½ pound 96 percent lean ground beef
- 2 medium tomatoes, chopped
- 1 onion, chopped
- 2 garlic cloves, minced
- 2 cups fresh baby spinach
- 2 tablespoons lemon juice
- ⅓ cup beef broth
- 2 tablespoons crumbled feta cheese

Directions:
1. In a 6-by-2-inch metal pan, crumble the beef.
2. Cook in the preheated Air Fryer for 7 minutes, stirring once during cooking, until browned.
3. Add the garlic, tomatoes, and onion to the pan.
4. Air-fry for 4 to 8 minutes more, or until the onion is tender.
5. Add the spinach, lemon juice, and beef broth.
6. Air-fry for 2 to 4 minutes more, or until the spinach is wilted.
7. Sprinkle with the feta cheese and serve immediately

Juicy Cheeseburger

Servings: 4 Servings
Cooking Time: 20 Minutes
Ingredients:
- 1 pound of 80/20 ground chuck beef
- 4 buns
- 4 slices of any cheese you like
- 1 ½ tablespoons of burger seasonings
- 1 teaspoon of Worcestershire sauce
- 1 teaspoon of liquid smoke
- Lettuce leaves, slices of tomatoes, onions, ketchup, for serving
- Pinch of salt and black pepper, to taste

Directions:
1. Preheat your air fryer to 360°F.
2. Add the ground beef, sauce, liquid smoke, seasonings, black pepper, and salt in a large mixing bowl. Mix it until smooth and make 4 patties.
3. Put the formed patties in the air fryer basket and cook at 360°F for 8 minutes. Flip them and cook for an extra 3–4 minutes.
4. Serve on buns* with ketchup, lettuce leaves, slices of onions, and tomatoes. Enjoy your Juicy Cheeseburger!

Beef And Spinach Rolls

Servings: 2
Cooking Time: 14 Minutes

Ingredients:

- 3 teaspoons pesto
- 2 pounds (907 g) beef flank steak
- 6 slices provolone cheese
- 3 ounces (85 g) roasted red bell peppers
- ¾ cup baby spinach
- 1 teaspoon sea salt
- 1 teaspoon black pepper

Directions:

1. Preheat the air fryer to 400°F (204°C).
2. Spoon equal amounts of the pesto onto each flank steak and spread it across evenly.
3. Put the cheese, roasted red peppers and spinach on top of the meat, about three-quarters of the way down.
4. Roll the steak up, holding it in place with toothpicks. Sprinkle with the sea salt and pepper.
5. Put inside the air fryer and air fry for 14 minutes, turning halfway through the cooking time.
6. Allow the beef to rest for 10 minutes before slicing up and serving.

Cheese Crusted Chops

Servings: 6
Cooking Time: 12 Minutes

Ingredients:

- ¼ teaspoon pepper
- ½ teaspoons salt
- 4 to 6 thick boneless pork chops
- 1 cup pork rind crumbs
- ¼ teaspoon chili powder
- ½ teaspoons onion powder
- 1 teaspoon smoked paprika
- 2 beaten eggs
- 3 tablespoons grated Parmesan cheese
- Cooking spray

Directions:

1. Preheat the air fryer to 400°F (205°C).
2. Rub the pepper and salt on both sides of pork chops.
3. In a food processor, pulse pork rinds into crumbs. Mix crumbs with chili powder, onion powder, and paprika in a bowl.
4. Beat eggs in another bowl.
5. Dip pork chops into eggs then into pork rind crumb mixture.
6. Spritz the air fryer with cooking spray and add pork chops to the basket.
7. Air fry for 12 minutes.
8. Serve garnished with the Parmesan cheese.

Homemade And Delectable Pork Chops

Servings: 4
Cooking Time: 9 Minutes
Ingredients:
- 4 pork chops, boneless
- 1 teaspoon onion powder
- 1 teaspoon smoked paprika
- ½ cup parmesan cheese, grated
- 2 tablespoons olive oil
- ½ teaspoon black pepper
- 1 teaspoon kosher salt

Directions:
1. Brush pork chops with olive oil.
2. In a suitable bowl, mix together parmesan cheese and spices.
3. Grease its air fryer basket with cooking spray.
4. Coat pork chops with parmesan cheese mixture and place in the air fryer basket.
5. Cook pork chops at 375 degrees F/ 190 degrees C for 9 minutes. Turn halfway through the cooking time.
6. Serve and enjoy.

Simple Pork Chops

Servings: 3
Cooking Time: 12 Minutes
Ingredients:
- 3 boneless pork chops
- Salt and pepper, to taste
- ½ cup all-purpose flour
- ½ cup breadcrumbs
- 1 tablespoon honey
- 2 tablespoons olive oil
- 1 tablespoon Dijon mustard
- 1 tablespoon soy sauce

Directions:
1. In a zip-lock bag, mix up the soy sauce, honey, olive oil, Dijon mustard and pork chops, then seal and refrigerate for 30 minutes.
2. After remove the pork chops from the marinade, season them with salt, pepper and coat them with flour and breadcrumbs.
3. Cook the pork chops in your air fryer at 370 degrees F/ 185 degrees C for 12 minutes.
4. When done, serve and enjoy.

Steak Fajitas With Vegetables

Servings: 6
Cooking Time: 15 Minutes
Ingredients:
- 1-pound steak, sliced
- 1 tablespoon olive oil
- 1 tablespoon fajita seasoning, gluten-free
- ½ cup onion, sliced
- 3 bell peppers, sliced

Directions:
1. Line air fryer basket with aluminum foil.
2. Add all the recipe ingredients suitable bowl and toss until well coated.
3. Transfer fajita mixture into the air fryer basket and cook at almost 390 degrees F/ 200 degrees C for 5 minutes.
4. Toss well and cook for 5-10 minutes more.
5. Serve and enjoy.

Unique Beef Cheeseburgers

Servings: 4
Cooking Time: 15 Minutes
Ingredients:
- ½ lb. ground beef
- ⅓ cup breadcrumbs
- 2 tablespoons parsley, finely chopped
- 3 tablespoons parmesan cheese, shredded
- ½ teaspoon salt
- ⅓ teaspoon pepper
- 4 slices Cheddar cheese
- 4 burger buns
- 1 red onion, sliced
- 4 romaine lettuce leaves
- 4 teaspoons mayonnaise
- 1 cup pickles, sliced

Directions:
1. Mix the ground beef with breadcrumbs, parmesan cheese, parsley, salt and pepper well in a suitable dish.
2. Form 4 patties from the meat mixture.
3. Cook the patties in your air fryer at 390 degrees F/ 200 degrees C for 13 minutes.
4. After that, place the cheese slices on the top and cook for 1 minute more.
5. When cooked, top with pickles, red onion, lettuce leaves, and mayonnaise.
6. Enjoy!

Beef Bites With Potatoes

Servings: 4 Servings
Cooking Time: 30 Minutes
Ingredients:
- 1 pound of ½-inch steak cubes
- ½ pound of potatoes
- 2 tablespoons of melted butter
- 1 teaspoon of Worcestershire sauce
- ½ teaspoon of garlic powder
- Pinch of salt and black pepper, to taste
- Minced parsley, for garnishing

Directions:
1. Cut the peeled potatoes into ½-inch pieces. Add them to a large pot and pour in water. Bring it to a boil and cook for 5 minutes until nearly tender.
2. Mix the steak cubes with potatoes in a large mixing bowl. Add in the melted butter, garlic powder, sauce, pepper, and salt. Mix it well.
3. Preheat your air fryer to 400°F.
4. Place the beef-potato mixture into the air fryer basket. Cook at 400°F for 13–18 minutes, flipping every 3–4 minutes.
5. Top with parsley and melted butter. Season with extra pepper or salt if desired.
6. Serve warm and enjoy your Beef Bites with Potatoes!

Korean Short Ribs

Servings: 4
Cooking Time: 10 Minutes
Ingredients:
- 8 (8-ounce) bone-in short ribs
- ½ cup soy sauce
- ¼ cup rice wine vinegar (see Substitution tip)
- ½ cup chopped onion
- 2 garlic cloves, minced
- 1 tablespoon sesame oil
- 1 teaspoon Sriracha
- 4 scallions, green parts (white parts optional), thinly sliced, divided
- Salt
- Pepper

Directions:
1. Place the short ribs in a sealable plastic bag. Add the soy sauce, rice wine vinegar, onion, garlic, sesame oil, Sriracha, and half of the scallions. Season with salt and pepper to taste.
2. Seal the bag and place it in the refrigerator to marinate for at least 1 hour; overnight is optimal.
3. Place the short ribs in the air fryer. Do not overfill. You may have to cook in two batches. Cook for 4 minutes.
4. Open the air fryer and flip the ribs. Cook for an additional 4 minutes.
5. If necessary, remove the cooked short ribs from the air fryer, then repeat steps 3 and 4 for the remaining ribs.
6. Sprinkle the short ribs with the remaining scallions, and serve.

Italian Lamb Chops With Avocado Mayo

Servings: 2
Cooking Time: 12 Minutes

Ingredients:

- 2 lamp chops
- 2 teaspoons Italian herbs
- 2 avocados
- ½ cup mayonnaise
- 1 tablespoon lemon juice

Directions:

1. Season the lamb chops with the Italian herbs, then set aside for 5 minutes.
2. Preheat the air fryer to 400°F (204°C) and place the rack inside.
3. Put the chops on the rack and air fry for 12 minutes.
4. In the meantime, halve the avocados and open to remove the pits. Spoon the flesh into a blender.
5. Add the mayonnaise and lemon juice and pulse until a smooth consistency is achieved.
6. Take care when removing the chops from the air fryer, then plate up and serve with the avocado mayo.

Cheesy Pork Chops

Servings: 2
Cooking Time: 8 Minutes

Ingredients:

- 4 pork chops
- ¼ cup cheddar cheese, shredded
- ½ teaspoon garlic powder
- ½ teaspoon salt

Directions:

1. At 350 degrees F/ 175 degrees C, preheat your air fryer.
2. Rub pork chops with garlic powder and salt and place in the air fryer basket.
3. Cook pork chops for 4 minutes.
4. Turn pork chops over and cook for 2 minutes.
5. Add cheese on top of pork chops and cook for 2 minutes more.
6. Serve and enjoy.

Pork Tenderloins

Servings: 3
Cooking Time: 30 Minutes
Ingredients:
- 1 teaspoon salt
- ½ teaspoon pepper
- 1 lb. pork tenderloin
- 2 tablespoons minced fresh rosemary
- 2 tablespoons olive oil, divided
- 1 garlic cloves, minced
- Apricot Glaze Ingredients:
- 1 cup apricot preserves
- 3 garlic cloves, minced
- 4 tablespoons lemon juice

Directions:
1. After mixing the pepper, salt, garlic, oil, and rosemary well, brush the pork with them on all sides.
2. If needed, you can cut pork crosswise in half.
3. Arrange the pork to the sprayed cooking pan and cook at 390 degrees F/ 200 degrees C for 3 minutes on each side.
4. While cooking the pork, mix all of the glaze ingredients well.
5. Baste the pork every 5 minutes.
6. Cook at 330 degrees F/ 165 degrees C and cook for 20 minutes more.
7. When done, serve and enjoy.

Peppercorn Crusted Beef Tenderloin

Servings:6
Cooking Time: 25 Minutes
Ingredients:
- 2 pounds (907 g) beef tenderloin
- 2 teaspoons roasted garlic, minced
- 2 tablespoons salted butter, melted
- 3 tablespoons ground 4-peppercorn blender

Directions:
1. Preheat the air fryer to 400°F (204°C).
2. Remove any surplus fat from the beef tenderloin.
3. Combine the roasted garlic and melted butter to apply to the tenderloin with a brush.
4. On a plate, spread out the peppercorns and roll the tenderloin in them, making sure they are covering and clinging to the meat.
5. Air fry the tenderloin in the air fryer for 25 minutes, turning halfway through cooking.
6. Let the tenderloin rest for ten minutes before slicing and serving.

Beef And Mushroom Calzones

Servings: 6
Cooking Time: 20 Minutes

Ingredients:
- Cooking oil
- ½ cup chopped onion
- 2 garlic cloves, minced
- ¼ cup chopped mushrooms
- 1 pound 93% lean ground beef
- 1 tablespoon Italian seasoning
- Salt
- Pepper
- 1½ cups pizza sauce
- 1 teaspoon all-purpose flour
- 1 (13-ounce) can refrigerated pizza dough
- 1 cup shredded Cheddar cheese

Directions:
1. Spray a skillet with cooking oil and place over medium-high heat. Add the chopped onion, garlic, and mushrooms. Cook for 2 to 3 minutes, until fragrant.
2. Add the ground beef, Italian seasoning, and salt and pepper to taste. Use a large spoon or spatula to break up the beef into small pieces. Cook for 2 to 4 minutes, until browned.
3. Add the pizza sauce. Stir to combine.
4. Sprinkle the flour on a flat work surface. Roll out the pizza dough. Cut the dough into 6 equal-sized rectangles.
5. Mound ½ cup of the ground beef mixture on each of the rectangles. Sprinkle 1 tablespoon of shredded cheese over the beef mixture.
6. Fold each crust up to close the calzones. Using the back of a fork, press along the open edges of each calzone to seal.
7. Place the calzones in the air fryer. Do not stack. Cook in batches. Spray the calzones with cooking oil. Cook for 10 minutes.
8. Remove the cooked calzones from the air fryer, then repeat step 7 for the remaining calzones.
9. Cool before serving.

Air Fried Ribeye Steak

Servings: 1
Cooking Time: 15 Minutes
Ingredients:

- 1 (1-pound / 454-g) ribeye steak
- Salt and ground black pepper, to taste
- 1 tablespoon peanut oil
- ½ tablespoon butter
- ½ teaspoon thyme, chopped

Directions:
1. Preheat a skillet in the air fryer at 400ºF (204ºC).
2. Season the steaks with salt and pepper. Remove the skillet from the air fryer once preheated.
3. Put the skillet on the stovetop burner on a medium heat and drizzle with the peanut oil.
4. Sear the steak for 2 minutes.
5. Turn over the steak and place in the air fryer for 6 minutes.
6. Take out the steak from the air fryer and place it back on the stove top on low heat to keep warm.
7. Toss in the butter and thyme and air fry for 3 minutes.
8. Rest for 5 minutes and serve.

Beef Steak Fingers

Servings: 4
Cooking Time: 8 Minutes
Ingredients:

- 4 small beef cube steaks
- Salt and ground black pepper, to taste
- ½ cup flour
- Cooking spray

Directions:
1. Preheat the air fryer to 390ºF (199ºC).
2. Cut cube steaks into 1-inch-wide strips.
3. Sprinkle lightly with salt and pepper to taste.
4. Roll in flour to coat all sides.
5. Spritz air fryer basket with cooking spray.
6. Put steak strips in air fryer basket in a single layer. Spritz top of steak strips with cooking spray.
7. Air fry for 4 minutes, turn strips over, and spritz with cooking spray.
8. Air fry 4 more minutes and test with fork for doneness. Steak fingers should be crispy outside with no red juices inside.
9. Repeat steps 5 through 7 to air fry remaining strips.
10. Serve immediately.

Air Fried Beef Ribs

Servings: 4
Cooking Time: 8 Minutes

Ingredients:
- 1 pound (454 g) meaty beef ribs, rinsed and drained
- 3 tablespoons apple cider vinegar
- 1 cup coriander, finely chopped
- 1 tablespoon fresh basil leaves, chopped
- 2 garlic cloves, finely chopped
- 1 chipotle powder
- 1 teaspoon fennel seeds
- 1 teaspoon hot paprika
- Kosher salt and black pepper, to taste
- ½ cup vegetable oil

Directions:
1. Coat the ribs with the remaining ingredients and refrigerate for at least 3 hours.
2. Preheat the air fryer to 360°F (182°C).
3. Separate the ribs from the marinade and put them on a grill pan. Air fry for 8 minutes.
4. Pour the remaining marinade over the ribs before serving.

Cheesy Beef Meatballs

Servings: 6
Cooking Time: 18 Minutes

Ingredients:
- 1 pound (454 g) ground beef
- ½ cup grated Parmesan cheese
- 1 tablespoon minced garlic
- ½ cup Mozzarella cheese
- 1 teaspoon freshly ground pepper

Directions:
1. Preheat the air fryer to 400°F (204°C).
2. In a bowl, mix all the ingredients together.
3. Roll the meat mixture into 5 generous meatballs.
4. Air fry inside the air fryer at 165°F (74°C) for about 18 minutes.
5. Serve immediately.

Sweet-and-sour Polish Sausage

Servings: 4
Cooking Time: 10 To 15 Minutes
Ingredients:
- ¾ pound Polish sausage
- 1 red bell pepper, cut into 1-inch strips
- ½ cup minced onion
- 3 tablespoons brown sugar
- ⅓ cup ketchup
- 2 tablespoons mustard
- 2 tablespoons apple cider vinegar
- ½ cup chicken broth

Directions:
1. Cut the sausage into 1½-inch pieces and put into a 6-inch metal bowl. Add the pepper and minced onion.
2. In a small bowl, combine the brown sugar, ketchup, mustard, apple cider vinegar, and chicken broth, and mix well. Pour into the bowl.
3. Roast for 10 to 15 minutes or until the sausage is hot, the vegetables tender, and the sauce bubbling and slightly thickened.
4. Did You Know? Polish sausage is almost always fully cooked when it is sold; read the label carefully to make sure you buy a fully cooked type for this recipe. Uncooked sausages are too fatty and release too much grease to cook in this appliance.

Barbecued Baby Back Ribs

Servings: 4
Cooking Time: 30 Minutes
Ingredients:
- 1 rack baby back ribs
- 1 teaspoon onion powder
- 1 teaspoon garlic powder
- 1 teaspoon brown sugar
- 1 teaspoon dried oregano
- Salt
- Pepper
- ½ cup barbecue sauce

Directions:
1. Use a sharp knife to remove the thin membrane from the back of the ribs. Cut the rack in half or as needed so that the ribs are able to fit in the air fryer.
2. In a small bowl, combine the onion powder, garlic powder, brown sugar, oregano, and salt and pepper to taste. Rub the seasoning onto the front and back of the ribs.
3. Cover the ribs with plastic wrap or foil and allow them to sit at room temperature for 30 minutes.
4. Place the ribs in the air fryer. It is okay to stack them. Cook for 15 minutes.
5. Open the air fryer. Flip the ribs. Cook for an additional 15 minutes.
6. Transfer the ribs to a serving dish. Drizzle the ribs with the barbecue sauce and serve.

Beef With Spanish Rice Casserole

Servings: 3
Cooking Time: 50 Minutes

Ingredients:

- ½-pound lean ground beef
- 2 tablespoons chopped green bell pepper
- 1 tablespoon chopped fresh cilantro
- ¼ cup shredded Cheddar cheese
- ½ teaspoon brown sugar
- ½ pinch ground pepper
- ⅓ cup uncooked long grain rice
- ¼ cup finely chopped onion
- ¼ cup chile sauce
- ¼ teaspoon ground cumin
- ¼ teaspoon Worcestershire sauce
- ½ (14.5 ounce) can canned tomatoes
- ½ cup water
- ½ teaspoon salt

Directions:

1. Spray the cooking pan of your air fryer with cooking spray.
2. Transfer the ground beef to the pan and cook at 360 degrees F/ 180 degrees C for 10 minutes.
3. After 5 minutes of cooking time, mix the crumble beef.
4. After discarding the excess fat, stir in pepper, Worcestershire sauce, salt, chile sauce, rice, cumin, brown sugar, water, tomatoes, green bell pepper, and onion.
5. Use the aluminum foil to cover the pan and cook for 25 minutes more, stirring regularly.
6. Stir at the end, press hard and sprinkle with cheese, then cook at 390 degrees F/ 200 degrees C for 15 minutes more or until the tops are lightly browned.
7. when done, serve with cilantro.

Fish And Seafood Recipes
Flavor Moroccan Harissa Shrimp

Servings: 3
Cooking Time: 10 Minutes
Ingredients:

- 1-pound breaded shrimp, frozen
- 1 teaspoon extra-virgin olive oil
- Sea salt, to taste
- Ground black pepper, to taste
- 1 teaspoon coriander seeds
- 1 teaspoon caraway seeds
- 1 teaspoon crushed red pepper
- 1 teaspoon fresh garlic, minced

Directions:
1. Arrange the breaded shrimp tossed with olive oil to the cooking basket and then arrange the basket to the air fryer.
2. Cook the shrimp at 400 degrees F/ 205 degrees C for 5 minutes.
3. After 5 minutes, shake the basket and cook an additional 4 minutes.
4. During cooking, mix the remaining ingredients until well combined.
5. Taste and adjust seasonings.
6. Toss the warm shrimp with the harissa sauce and serve immediately. Enjoy!

Sesame-glazed Salmon

Servings: 4
Cooking Time: 16 Minutes
Ingredients:

- 3 tablespoons soy sauce
- 1 tablespoon rice wine or dry sherry
- 1 tablespoon brown sugar
- 1 tablespoon toasted sesame oil
- 1 teaspoon minced garlic
- ¼ teaspoon minced ginger
- 4 (6 ounce) salmon fillets, skin-on
- Olive oil
- ½ tablespoon sesame seeds

Directions:
1. In a small bowl, mix together the soy sauce, rice wine, brown sugar, toasted sesame oil, garlic, and ginger.
2. Place the salmon in a shallow baking dish and pour the marinade over the fillets. Cover and refrigerate for at least 1 hour, turning the fillets occasionally to coat in the marinade.
3. Spray a fryer basket lightly with olive oil.
4. Shake off as much marinade as possible and place the fillets, skin side down, in the fryer basket in a single layer. Reserve the marinade. You may need to cook them in batches.
5. Air fry for 8 to 10 minutes. Brush the tops of the salmon fillets with the reserved marinade and sprinkle with sesame seeds.
6. Increase the fryer temperature to 400°F and cook for 2 to 5 more minutes for medium, 1 to 3 minutes for medium rare, or 4 to 6 minutes for well done.

Cajun Lemon Branzino

Servings: 4
Cooking Time: 8 Minutes

Ingredients:

- 1-pound branzino, trimmed, washed
- 1 teaspoon Cajun seasoning
- 1 tablespoon sesame oil
- 1 tablespoon lemon juice
- 1 teaspoon salt

Directions:

1. Carefully coat the branzino with salt and Cajun seasoning.
2. Drizzle the lemon juice and sesame oil over the branzino.
3. At 380 degrees F/ 195 degrees C, heat your air fryer in advance.
4. Place the branzino in the air fryer and cook it for 8 minutes at 380 degrees F/ 195 degrees C.
5. When done, serve and enjoy.

Tuna And Fruit Kebabs

Servings: 4
Cooking Time: 8 To 12 Minutes

Ingredients:

- 1 pound tuna steaks, cut into 1-inch cubes
- ½ cup canned pineapple chunks, drained, juice reserved
- ½ cup large red grapes
- 1 tablespoon honey
- 2 teaspoons grated fresh ginger
- 1 teaspoon olive oil
- Pinch cayenne pepper

Directions:

1. Thread the tuna, pineapple, and grapes on 8 bamboo (see Tip) or 4 metal skewers that fit in the air fryer.
2. In a small bowl, whisk the honey, 1 tablespoon of reserved pineapple juice, the ginger, olive oil, and cayenne. Brush this mixture over the kebabs. Let them stand for 10 minutes.
3. Grill the kebabs for 8 to 12 minutes, or until the tuna reaches an internal temperature of at least 145°F on a meat thermometer, and the fruit is tender and glazed, brushing once with the remaining sauce. Discard any remaining marinade. Serve immediately.

Creamy Savory Salmon

Servings: 4
Cooking Time: 25 Minutes
Ingredients:
- For salmon:
- 2 teaspoons olive oil
- 24-ounce (4 pieces) salmon
- 1 pinch salt
- For the sauce:
- ½ cup sour cream
- ½ cup non-fat: Greek yogurt
- 1 pinch salt
- 2 tablespoons dill, finely chopped

Directions:
1. Make the salmon pieces of 6 ounces each, brush the pieces with olive oil and then top them with salt.
2. Place the pieces in the basket that has been coated with cooking oil or spray.
3. Arrange the basket to the air fryer and cook at 270 degrees F/ 130 degrees C for 20-25 minutes.
4. In a bowl of medium size, thoroughly mix the sauce ingredients.
5. When the pieces has finished, serve warm with the sauce!

Fish Mania With Mustard

Servings: 4-5
Cooking Time: 10 Minutes
Ingredients:
- 1 cup soft bread crumbs
- 1 teaspoon whole-grain mustard
- 2 cans canned fish
- 2 celery stalks, chopped
- 1 egg, whisked
- ½ teaspoon sea salt
- ¼ teaspoon black peppercorns, cracked
- 1 teaspoon paprika

Directions:
1. Thoroughly mix the fish, breadcrumbs, celery and other ingredients in a large bowl.
2. Make four cakes shapes from the mixture and refrigerate for 45-50 minutes.
3. Place the cakes in the basket that has been coated with cooking oil or spray.
4. Arrange it to air fryer and cook for 5 minutes at 360 degrees F/ 180 degrees C.
5. After 5 minutes, flip the cakes gently and cook for another 4 minutes
6. Serve over mashed potatoes.

Old Bay Cod Fish Fillets

Servings: 2
Cooking Time: 12 Minutes

Ingredients:
- 2 cod fish fillets
- 1 teaspoon butter, melted
- 1 teaspoon Old Bay seasoning
- 1 egg, beaten
- 2 tablespoons coconut milk, unsweetened
- ⅓ cup coconut flour, unsweetened

Directions:
1. Prepare a Ziploc bag, add the cod fish fillets, butter and Old Bay seasoning, shake to coat the fillets well on all sides.
2. Whisk the egg and coconut milk until frothy in a shallow bowl.
3. In another bowl, place the coconut flour.
4. Coat the fish fillets with the egg mixture and coconut flour in order, pressing to adhere.
5. Cook the fish fillets at 390 degrees F/ 200 degrees C until the fish fillets flake easily when poking it with a fork, for 12 minutes.
6. Flip halfway through.
7. Bon appétit!

Trimmed Mackerel With Spring Onions

Servings: 5
Cooking Time: 20 Minutes

Ingredients:
- 1 pound mackerel, trimmed
- 1 tablespoon ground paprika
- 1 green bell pepper
- ½ cup spring onions, chopped
- 1 tablespoon avocado oil
- 1 teaspoon apple cider vinegar
- ½-teaspoon salt

Directions:
1. Sprinkle the clean mackerel with ground paprika.
2. Chop the green bell pepper.
3. Fill the mackerel with bell pepper and spring onion.
4. After this, sprinkle the fish with avocado oil, salt and apple cider vinegar.
5. At 375 degrees F/ 190 degrees C, heat your air fryer in advance.
6. Place the mackerel in the basket and arrange the basket to the air fryer.
7. Cook the mackerel for 20 minutes at 375 degrees F/ 190 degrees C.
8. When cooked, serve and enjoy.

Spiced Catfish Fillets

Servings: 4
Cooking Time: 7 Minutes
Ingredients:
- 1 lb. catfish fillets
- 1 tablespoon olive oil
- 1 teaspoon paprika
- 1 teaspoon garlic powder
- 1 teaspoon dried basil
- 1 tablespoon Jamaican allspice, ground
- ½ lemon, juiced

Directions:
1. At 390 degrees F/ 200 degrees C, preheat your air fryer.
2. Grease its air fryer basket with cooking spray.
3. In a suitable bowl, mix paprika, garlic powder, and Jamaican allspice seasoning.
4. Rub the catfish fillets with the spice mixture.
5. Transfer to the cooking basket and drizzle the olive oil.
6. Cook for 7 minutes, slide out the air fryer basket and turn the fillets; cook further for 6 minutes.
7. Serve sprinkled with lemon juice.

Clams With Spring Onions

Servings: 4
Cooking Time: 20 Minutes
Ingredients:
- 15 small clams
- 1 tablespoon spring onions, chopped
- Juice of 1 lime
- 10 oz. coconut cream
- 1 tablespoon cilantro, chopped
- 1 teaspoon olive oil

Directions:
1. Heat up a suitable pan that fits your air fryer with the oil over medium heat, add the spring onions and sauté for 2 minutes.
2. Add lime juice, coconut cream and the cilantro, stir and cook for 2 minutes more.
3. Add the clams, toss, introduce in the fryer and cook at 390 degrees F/ 200 degrees C for 15 minutes.
4. Divide into bowls and serve hot.

Cilantro-lime Fried Shrimp

Servings: 4
Cooking Time: 10 Minutes
Ingredients:

- 1 pound raw shrimp, peeled and deveined with tails on or off (see Prep tip)
- ½ cup chopped fresh cilantro
- Juice of 1 lime
- 1 egg
- ½ cup all-purpose flour
- ¾ cup bread crumbs
- Salt
- Pepper
- Cooking oil
- ½ cup cocktail sauce (optional)

Directions:
1. Place the shrimp in a plastic bag and add the cilantro and lime juice. Seal the bag. Shake to combine. Marinate in the refrigerator for 30 minutes.
2. In a small bowl, beat the egg. In another small bowl, place the flour. Place the bread crumbs in a third small bowl, and season with salt and pepper to taste.
3. Spray the air fryer basket with cooking oil.
4. Remove the shrimp from the plastic bag. Dip each in the flour, then the egg, and then the bread crumbs.
5. Place the shrimp in the air fryer. It is okay to stack them. Spray the shrimp with cooking oil. Cook for 4 minutes.
6. Open the air fryer and flip the shrimp. I recommend flipping individually instead of shaking to keep the breading intact. Cook for an additional 4 minutes, or until crisp.
7. Cool before serving. Serve with cocktail sauce if desired.

Pesto Fish Finger Sandwich

Servings: 4
Cooking Time: 15 Minutes
Ingredients:

- 4 finger fish fillets
- 2 tablespoons flour
- 10 capers
- 4 bread rolls
- 2 ounces breadcrumbs
- 4 tablespoons pesto sauce
- 4 lettuce leaves
- Black pepper and salt, to taste

Directions:
1. At 370 degrees F/ 185 degrees C, preheat your air fryer.
2. Season the finger fish fillets with black pepper and salt, and coat them with the dry flour first; then dip in the breadcrumbs.
3. Arrange the fillets onto a baking mat and cook in the air fryer for almost 10 to 15 minutes.
4. Cut the bread rolls in half.
5. Place a lettuce leaf on top of the bottom halves; put the fillets over.
6. Spread a tablespoon of pesto sauce on top of each fillet, and top with the remaining halves.
7. Serve.

Salmon Patties

Servings: 2 Servings
Cooking Time: 25 Minutes

Ingredients:

- 2 (7.5-oz) cans of unsalted pink salmon
- ½ cup of panko bread crumbs
- 1 large egg
- 2 tablespoons of mayonnaise
- 2 tablespoons of chopped fresh dill
- 2 teaspoons of mustard
- Lime wedges, for serving
- Pinch of black pepper and salt, to taste

Directions:

1. Preheat your air fryer to 400ºF. Spray some oil inside the air fryer basket.
2. Drain water from the salmon, remove skin and large bones, put it in a medium bowl. Add in bread crumbs, mayonnaise, egg, mustard, pepper, and dill. Mix it well until combined. Form 4 same-sized patties.*
3. Put the patties in the air fryer basket in a single layer; avoid them touching. Cook at 400ºF for 6 minutes, gently flip them, and cook for another 6 minutes until browned.
4. Serve warm with lemon wedges and enjoy your Salmon Patties!

Glazed Fillets

Servings: 4
Cooking Time: 15 Minutes

Ingredients:

- 4 flounder fillets
- 1 ½ tablespoons dark sesame oil
- 2 tablespoons sake
- Sea salt and cracked mixed peppercorns, as needed
- ¼ cup soy sauce
- 1 teaspoon brown sugar
- 1 tablespoon grated lemon rind
- 2 garlic cloves, minced
- Fresh chopped chives, to serve

Directions:

1. To marinate, prepare a large deep dish, add the ingredients except for chives and stir a little. Cover and refrigerate for 2-3 hours.
2. Add the fish to the basket that has been coated with the cooking oil or spray.
3. Arrange it to the air fryer and cook at 360 degrees F/ 180 degrees C for 12 minutes, flipping halfway through.
4. Pour the remaining marinade into a saucepan; simmer over medium-low heat until it has thickened.
5. Serve the fish with the marinade and chives on top!

Lemon-pepper Tilapia With Garlic Aioli

Servings: 4
Cooking Time: 15 Minutes

Ingredients:

- For the tilapia
- 4 tilapia fillets (see Prep tip)
- 1 tablespoon extra-virgin olive oil
- 1 teaspoon paprika
- 1 teaspoon garlic powder
- 1 teaspoon dried basil
- Lemon-pepper seasoning (such as McCormick Perfect Pinch Lemon & Pepper Seasoning)
- For the garlic aioli
- 2 garlic cloves, minced
- 1 tablespoon mayonnaise
- 1 teaspoon extra-virgin olive oil
- Juice of ½ lemon
- Salt
- Pepper

Directions:

1. Coat the fish with the olive oil. Season with the paprika, garlic powder, dried basil, and lemon-pepper seasoning.
2. Place the fish in the air fryer. It is okay to stack the fish. Cook for 8 minutes.
3. Open the air fryer and flip the fish. Cook for an additional 7 minutes.
4. In a small bowl, combine the garlic, mayonnaise, olive oil, lemon juice, and salt and pepper to taste. Whisk well to combine.
5. Serve alongside the fish.

Red Snapper With Hot Chili Paste

Servings: 4
Cooking Time: 15 Minutes

Ingredients:

- 4 red snapper fillets, boneless
- A pinch of salt and black pepper
- 2 garlic cloves, minced
- 1 tablespoon coconut aminos
- 1 tablespoon lime juice
- 1 tablespoon hot chili paste
- 1 tablespoon olive oil

Directions:

1. In addition to the fish, mix up the other ingredients in a bowl and stir well.
2. Use the mixture to rub the fish, then place the fish in the basket of your air fryer.
3. Cook for 15 minutes at 380 degrees F/ 195 degrees C.
4. Serve with a side salad.

Beer Squid

Servings: 3
Cooking Time: 20 Minutes

Ingredients:
- 1 cup beer
- 1 lb. squid
- 1 cup all-purpose flour
- 2 eggs
- ½ cup cornstarch
- Sea salt, to taste
- ½-teaspoon ground black pepper
- 1 tablespoon Old Bay seasoning

Directions:
1. At 390 degrees F/ 200 degrees C, heat your air fryer in advance.
2. Clean the squid and then cut them into rings. Add the beer and squid in a glass bowl, cover and let it sit in your refrigerator for 1 hour.
3. Rinse the squid before patting it dry.
4. Add the flour in a shallow bowl; in another bowl, whisk the eggs. Lastly, in a third shallow bowl, add the cornstarch and seasonings.
5. Dredge the calamari in the flour.
6. Then dip the rings into the egg mixture and coat them with the cornstarch on all sided.
7. Arrange them in the cooking basket. Spritz with cooking oil and cook for 9 to 12 minutes, depending on the desired level of doneness. Work in batches.
8. Serve warm with your favorite dipping sauce. Enjoy!

Garlic Shrimp

Servings: 2 Servings
Cooking Time: 20 Minutes

Ingredients:
- 1 pound of peeled raw shrimp
- ¼ teaspoon of garlic powder
- Olive oil, to coat
- Pinch of salt, black pepper, and chili flakes, to taste
- Minced cilantro, for garnishing
- Lemon wedges, for serving

Directions:
1. Preheat your air fryer to 400°F.
2. Add the shrimp, garlic powder, oil, pepper, and salt to a mixing bowl. Mix it until all shrimp are coated. Transfer the shrimp in the preheated air fryer basket in a single layer.
3. Cook at 400°F for 10–14 minutes, stirring and flipping occasionally.
4. Serve warm with lemon wedges. Top with minced cilantro and chili flakes. Enjoy your Garlic Shrimp!

Salmon On Bed Of Fennel And Carrot

Servings: 2
Cooking Time:13 To 14 Minutes
Ingredients:
- 1 fennel bulb, thinly sliced
- 1 large carrot, peeled and sliced
- 1 small onion, thinly sliced
- ¼ cup low-fat sour cream
- ¼ teaspoon coarsely ground pepper
- 2 (5 ounce) salmon fillets

Directions:
1. Combine the fennel, carrot, and onion in a bowl and toss.
2. Put the vegetable mixture into a 6-inch metal pan. Roast in the air fryer for 4 minutes or until the vegetables are crisp tender.
3. Remove the pan from the air fryer. Stir in the sour cream and sprinkle the vegetables with the pepper.
4. Top with the salmon fillets.
5. Return the pan to the air fryer. Roast for another 9 to 10 minutes or until the salmon just barely flakes when tested with a fork.

Baked Sardines

Servings: 3
Cooking Time: 40 Minutes
Ingredients:
- 1-pound fresh sardines
- Sea salt, to taste
- Ground black pepper, to taste
- 1 teaspoon Italian seasoning mix
- 2 cloves garlic, minced
- 3 tablespoons olive oil
- ½ lemon, freshly squeezed

Directions:
1. Toss salt, black pepper, Italian seasoning mix and the sardines well.
2. Cook the sardines in your air fryer at 325 degrees F/ 160 degrees C for 35 to 40 minutes or until skin is crispy.
3. To make the sauce, whisk the remaining ingredients.
4. Serve warm sardines with the sauce on the side. Bon appétit!

Tasty Juicy Salmon

Servings: 2
Cooking Time: 13 Minutes
Ingredients:
- 2 salmon fillets
- 4 asparagus stalks
- ¼ cup champagne
- Salt and black pepper, to taste
- ¼ cup white sauce
- 1½ teaspoon olive oil

Directions:
1. Heat the air fryer ahead of time.
2. In a bowl, mix the salmon fillets, asparagus, champagne, salt, black pepper, white sauce, and olive oil together and divide this mixture evenly over 2 foil papers.
3. Arrange the foil papers in the basket of your air fryer and cook for about 13 minutes at 355 degrees F/ 180 degrees C.
4. Dish out in a platter and serve hot.

Sea Bream Fillet With Tomato Sauce

Servings: 4
Cooking Time: 8 Minutes
Ingredients:
- 1 tablespoon keto tomato sauce
- 1 tablespoon avocado oil
- 1 teaspoon ground black pepper
- ½-teaspoon salt
- 12 oz. sea bream fillet

Directions:
1. Cut the sea bream fillet on 4 servings.
2. After that, mix up tomato sauce, avocado oil, salt, and ground black pepper in a mixing bowl.
3. Rub the fish fillets with tomato mixture on both sides.
4. Line the air fryer basket with foil.
5. Put the sea bream fillets on the foil and cook them for 8 minutes at 390 degrees F/ 200 degrees C.

Vegetarians Recipes
Rice & Bean Burritos

Servings: 4
Cooking Time: 20 Minutes
Ingredients:

- 1 bell pepper, sliced
- ½ red onion, thinly sliced
- 2 garlic cloves, peeled
- 1 tbsp olive oil
- 1 cup cooked brown rice
- 1 can pinto beans
- ½ tsp salt
- ¼ tsp chili powder
- ¼ tsp ground cumin
- ¼ tsp smoked paprika
- 1 tbsp lime juice
- 4 tortillas
- 2 tsp grated Parmesan cheese
- 1 avocado, diced
- 4 tbsp salsa
- 2 tbsp chopped cilantro

Directions:
1. Preheat air fryer to 400°F. Combine bell pepper, onion, garlic, and olive oil. Place in the frying basket and Roast for 5 minutes. Shake and roast for another 5 minutes.
2. Remove the garlic from the basket and mince finely. Add to a large bowl along with brown rice, pinto beans, salt, chili powder, cumin, paprika, and lime juice. Divide the roasted vegetable mixture between the tortillas. Top with rice mixture, Parmesan, avocado, cilantro, and salsa. Fold in the sides, then roll the tortillas over the filling. Serve.

Hearty Salad

Servings: 2
Cooking Time: 15 Minutes
Ingredients:

- 5 oz cauliflower, cut into florets
- 2 grated carrots
- 1 tbsp olive oil
- 1 tbsp lemon juice
- 2 tbsp raisins
- 2 tbsp roasted pepitas
- 2 tbsp diced red onion
- ¼ cup mayonnaise
- 1/8 tsp black pepper
- 1 tsp cumin
- ½ tsp chia seeds
- ½ tsp sesame seeds

Directions:
1. Preheat air fryer at 350°F. Combine the cauliflower, cumin, olive oil, black pepper and lemon juice in a bowl, place it in the frying basket, and Bake for 5 minutes. Transfer it to a serving dish. Toss in the remaining ingredients. Let chill covered in the fridge until ready to use. Serve sprinkled with sesame and chia seeds.

Black Bean Empanadas

Servings: 12
Cooking Time: 35 Minutes

Ingredients:

- 1½ cups all-purpose flour
- 1 cup whole-wheat flour
- 1 teaspoon salt
- ½ cup cold unsalted butter
- 1 egg
- ½ cup milk
- One 14.5-ounce can black beans, drained and rinsed
- ¼ cup chopped cilantro
- 1 cup shredded purple cabbage
- 1 cup shredded Monterey jack cheese
- ¼ cup salsa

Directions:

1. In a food processor, place the all-purpose flour, whole-wheat flour, salt, and butter into processor and process for 2 minutes, scraping down the sides of the food processor every 30 seconds. Add in the egg and blend for 30 seconds. Using the pulse button, add in the milk 1 tablespoon at a time, or until dough is moist enough to handle and be rolled into a ball. Let the dough rest at room temperature for 30 minutes.
2. Meanwhile, in a large bowl, mix together the black beans, cilantro, cabbage, Monterey Jack cheese, and salsa.
3. On a floured surface, cut the dough in half; then form a ball and cut each ball into 6 equal pieces, totaling 12 equal pieces. Work with one piece at a time, and cover the remaining dough with a towel.
4. Roll out a piece of dough into a 6-inch round, much like a tortilla, ¼ inch thick. Place 4 tablespoons of filling in the center of the round, and fold over to form a half-circle. Using a fork, crimp the edges together and pierce the top for air holes. Repeat with the remaining dough and filling.
5. Preheat the air fryer to 350°F.
6. Working in batches, place 3 to 4 empanadas in the air fryer basket and spray with cooking spray. Cook for 4 minutes, flip over the empanadas and spray with cooking spray, and cook another 4 minutes.

Cheesy Enchilada Stuffed Baked Potatoes

Servings: 4
Cooking Time: 37 Minutes

Ingredients:
- 2 medium russet potatoes, washed
- One 15-ounce can mild red enchilada sauce
- One 15-ounce can low-sodium black beans, rinsed and drained
- 1 teaspoon taco seasoning
- ½ cup shredded cheddar cheese
- 1 medium avocado, halved
- ½ teaspoon garlic powder
- ¼ teaspoon black pepper
- ¼ teaspoon salt
- 2 teaspoons fresh lime juice
- 2 tablespoon chopped red onion
- ¼ cup chopped cilantro

Directions:
1. Preheat the air fryer to 390°F.
2. Puncture the outer surface of the potatoes with a fork.
3. Set the potatoes inside the air fryer basket and cook for 20 minutes, rotate, and cook another 10 minutes.
4. In a large bowl, mix the enchilada sauce, black beans, and taco seasoning.
5. When the potatoes have finished cooking, carefully remove them from the air fryer basket and let cool for 5 minutes.
6. Using a pair of tongs to hold the potato if it's still too hot to touch, slice the potato in half lengthwise. Use a spoon to scoop out the potato flesh and add it into the bowl with the enchilada sauce. Mash the potatoes with the enchilada sauce mixture, creating a uniform stuffing.
7. Place the potato skins into an air-fryer-safe pan and stuff the halves with the enchilada stuffing. Sprinkle the cheese over the top of each potato.
8. Set the air fryer temperature to 350°F, return the pan to the air fryer basket, and cook for another 5 to 7 minutes to heat the potatoes and melt the cheese.
9. While the potatoes are cooking, take the avocado and scoop out the flesh into a small bowl. Mash it with the back of a fork; then mix in the garlic powder, pepper, salt, lime juice, and onion. Set aside.
10. When the potatoes have finished cooking, remove the pan from the air fryer and place the potato halves on a plate. Top with avocado mash and fresh cilantro. Serve immediately.

Vegetarian Stuffed Bell Peppers

Servings: 3
Cooking Time: 40 Minutes
Ingredients:
- 1 cup mushrooms, chopped
- 1 tbsp allspice
- ¾ cup Alfredo sauce
- ½ cup canned diced tomatoes
- 1 cup cooked rice
- 2 tbsp dried parsley
- 2 tbsp hot sauce
- Salt and pepper to taste
- 3 large bell peppers

Directions:
1. Preheat air fryer to 375°F. Whisk mushrooms, allspice and 1 cup of boiling water until smooth. Stir in Alfredo sauce, tomatoes and juices, rice, parsley, hot sauce, salt, and black pepper. Set aside. Cut the top of each bell pepper, take out the core and seeds without breaking the pepper. Fill each pepper with the rice mixture and cover them with a 6-inch square of aluminum foil, folding the edges. Roast for 30 minutes until tender. Let cool completely before unwrapping. Serve immediately.

Black Bean Stuffed Potato Boats

Servings: 4
Cooking Time: 55 Minutes
Ingredients:
- 4 russets potatoes
- 1 cup chipotle mayonnaise
- 1 cup canned black beans
- 2 tomatoes, chopped
- 1 scallion, chopped
- 1/3 cup chopped cilantro
- 1 poblano chile, minced
- 1 avocado, diced

Directions:
1. Preheat air fryer to 390°F. Clean the potatoes, poke with a fork, and spray with oil. Put in the air fryer and Bake for 30 minutes or until softened.
2. Heat the beans in a pan over medium heat. Put the potatoes on a plate and cut them across the top. Open them with a fork so you can stuff them. Top each potato with chipotle mayonnaise, beans, tomatoes, scallions, cilantro, poblano chile, and avocado. Serve immediately.

Meatless Kimchi Bowls

Servings: 4
Cooking Time: 20 Minutes
Ingredients:
- 2 cups canned chickpeas
- 1 carrot, julienned
- 6 scallions, sliced
- 1 zucchini, diced
- 2 tbsp coconut aminos
- 2 tsp sesame oil
- 1 tsp rice vinegar
- 2 tsp granulated sugar
- 1 tbsp gochujang
- ¼ tsp salt
- ½ cup kimchi
- 2 tsp roasted sesame seeds

Directions:
1. Preheat air fryer to 350°F. Combine all ingredients, except for the kimchi, 2 scallions, and sesame seeds, in a baking pan. Place the pan in the frying basket and Air Fry for 6 minutes. Toss in kimchi and cook for 2 more minutes. Divide between 2 bowls and garnish with the remaining scallions and sesame seeds. Serve immediately.

Crispy Avocados With Pico De Gallo

Servings: 2
Cooking Time: 15 Minutes
Ingredients:
- 1 cup diced tomatoes
- 1 tbsp lime juice
- 1 tsp lime zest
- 2 tbsp chopped cilantro
- 1 serrano chiles, minced
- 2 cloves garlic, minced
- 1 tbsp diced white onions
- ½ tsp salt
- 2 avocados, halved and pitted
- 4 tbsp cheddar shreds

Directions:
1. Preheat air fryer to 350°F. Combine all ingredients, except for avocados and cheddar cheese, in a bowl and let chill covered in the fridge. Place avocado halves, cut sides-up, in the frying basket, scatter cheese shreds over top of avocado halves, and Air Fry for 4 minutes. Top with pico de gallo and serve.

Corn On The Cob

Servings: 2–4 Servings
Cooking Time: 20 Minutes

Ingredients:
- 2–4 ears of cleaned fresh corn
- 2 tablespoons of butter
- Pinch of salt and black pepper, to taste

Directions:
1. Preheat your air fryer to 370°F. Spray some oil inside the air fryer basket.
2. Wash the corn and dry them with a paper towel. Cut the corn in half to fit the size of the air fryer basket.
3. Grease all sides of corn with the melted butter. Season generously with pepper and salt around all sides of the corn.
4. Put in the air fryer and cook at 370°F for 12–16 minutes*, flipping halfway, until lightly browned and tender.
5. Top with grated Parmesan cheese and nutritional yeast for extra flavor.
6. Serve warm and enjoy your Corn on the Cob!

Nutrition:
- al yeast, grated Parmesan cheese, for serving

Gorgeous Jalapeño Poppers

Servings: 6
Cooking Time: 25 Minutes

Ingredients:
- 6 center-cut bacon slices, halved
- 6 jalapeños, halved lengthwise
- 4 oz cream cheese
- ¼ cup grated Gruyere cheese
- 2 tbsp chives, chopped

Directions:
1. Scoop out seeds and membranes of the jalapeño halves, discard. Combine cream cheese, Gruyere cheese, and chives in a bowl. Fill the jalapeño halves with the cream cheese filling using a small spoon. Wrap each pepper with a slice of bacon and secure with a toothpick.
2. Preheat air fryer to 325°F. Put the stuffed peppers in a single layer on the greased frying basket and Bake until the peppers are tender, cheese is melted, and the bacon is brown, 11-13minutes. Serve warm and enjoy!

Pizza Portobello Mushrooms

Servings: 2
Cooking Time: 18 Minutes

Ingredients:

- 2 portobello mushroom caps, gills removed (see Figure 13-1)
- 1 teaspoon extra-virgin olive oil
- ¼ cup diced onion
- 1 teaspoon minced garlic
- 1 medium zucchini, shredded
- 1 teaspoon dried oregano
- ½ teaspoon black pepper
- ¼ teaspoon salt
- ⅓ cup marinara sauce
- ¼ cup shredded part-skim mozzarella cheese
- ¼ teaspoon red pepper flakes
- 2 tablespoons Parmesan cheese
- 2 tablespoons chopped basil

Directions:

1. Preheat the air fryer to 370°F.
2. Lightly spray the mushrooms with an olive oil mist and place into the air fryer to cook for 10 minutes, cap side up.
3. Add the olive oil to a pan and sauté the onion and garlic together for about 2 to 4 minutes. Stir in the zucchini, oregano, pepper, and salt, and continue to cook. When the zucchini has cooked down (usually about 4 to 6 minutes), add in the marinara sauce. Remove from the heat and stir in the mozzarella cheese.
4. Remove the mushrooms from the air fryer basket when cooking completes. Reset the temperature to 350°F.
5. Using a spoon, carefully stuff the mushrooms with the zucchini marinara mixture.
6. Return the stuffed mushrooms to the air fryer basket and cook for 5 to 8 minutes, or until the cheese is lightly browned. You should be able to easily insert a fork into the mushrooms when they're cooked.
7. Remove the mushrooms and sprinkle the red pepper flakes, Parmesan cheese, and fresh basil over the top.
8. Serve warm.

Broccoli Cheddar Stuffed Potatoes

Servings: 2
Cooking Time: 42 Minutes

Ingredients:

- 2 large russet potatoes, scrubbed
- 1 tablespoon olive oil
- salt and freshly ground black pepper
- 2 tablespoons butter
- ¼ cup sour cream
- 3 tablespoons half-and-half (or milk)
- 1¼ cups grated Cheddar cheese, divided
- ¾ teaspoon salt
- freshly ground black pepper
- 1 cup frozen baby broccoli florets, thawed and drained

Directions:

1. Preheat the air fryer to 400°F.
2. Rub the potatoes all over with olive oil and season generously with salt and freshly ground black pepper. Transfer the potatoes into the air fryer basket and air-fry for 30 minutes, turning the potatoes over halfway through the cooking process.
3. Remove the potatoes from the air fryer and let them rest for 5 minutes. Cut a large oval out of the top of both potatoes. Leaving half an inch of potato flesh around the edge of the potato, scoop the inside of the potato out and into a large bowl to prepare the potato filling. Mash the scooped potato filling with a fork and add the butter, sour cream, half-and-half, 1 cup of the grated Cheddar cheese, salt and pepper to taste. Mix well and then fold in the broccoli florets.
4. Stuff the hollowed out potato shells with the potato and broccoli mixture. Mound the filling high in the potatoes – you will have more filling than room in the potato shells.
5. Transfer the stuffed potatoes back to the air fryer basket and air-fry at 360°F for 10 minutes. Sprinkle the remaining Cheddar cheese on top of each stuffed potato, lower the heat to 330°F and air-fry for an additional minute or two to melt cheese.

Quinoa Burgers With Feta Cheese And Dill

Servings: 6
Cooking Time: 10 Minutes

Ingredients:

- 1 cup quinoa (red, white or multi-colored)
- 1½ cups water
- 1 teaspoon salt
- freshly ground black pepper
- 1½ cups rolled oats
- 3 eggs, lightly beaten
- ¼ cup minced white onion
- ½ cup crumbled feta cheese
- ¼ cup chopped fresh dill
- salt and freshly ground black pepper
- vegetable or canola oil, in a spray bottle
- whole-wheat hamburger buns (or gluten-free hamburger buns*)
- arugula
- tomato, sliced
- red onion, sliced
- mayonnaise

Directions:

1. Make the quinoa: Rinse the quinoa in cold water in a saucepan, swirling it with your hand until any dry husks rise to the surface. Drain the quinoa as well as you can and then put the saucepan on the stovetop to dry and toast the quinoa. Turn the heat to medium-high and shake the pan regularly until you see the quinoa moving easily and can hear the seeds moving in the pan, indicating that they are dry. Add the water, salt and pepper. Bring the liquid to a boil and then reduce the heat to low or medium-low. You should see just a few bubbles, not a boil. Cover with a lid, leaving it askew and simmer for 20 minutes. Turn the heat off and fluff the quinoa with a fork. If there's any liquid left in the bottom of the pot, place it back on the burner for another 3 minutes or so. Spread the cooked quinoa out on a sheet pan to cool.
2. Combine the room temperature quinoa in a large bowl with the oats, eggs, onion, cheese and dill. Season with salt and pepper and mix well (remember that feta cheese is salty). Shape the mixture into 6 patties with flat sides (so they fit more easily into the air fryer). Add a little water or a few more rolled oats if necessary to get the mixture to be the right consistency to make patties.
3. Preheat the air-fryer to 400°F.
4. Spray both sides of the patties generously with oil and transfer them to the air fryer basket in one layer (you will probably have to cook these burgers in batches, depending on the size of your air fryer). Air-fry each batch at 400°F for 10 minutes, flipping the burgers over halfway through the cooking time.
5. Build your burger on the whole-wheat hamburger buns with arugula, tomato, red onion and mayonnaise.

Sweet Roasted Carrots

Servings: 4
Cooking Time: 25 Minutes
Ingredients:
- 6 carrots, cut into ½-inch pieces
- 2 tbsp butter, melted
- 2 tbsp parsley, chopped
- 1 tsp honey

Directions:
1. Preheat air fryer to 390°F. Add carrots to a baking pan and pour over butter, honey, and 2-3 tbsp of water. Mix well. Transfer the carrots to the greased frying basket and Roast for 12 minutes, shaking the basket once. Sprinkle with parsley and serve warm.

Cheddar Bean Taquitos

Servings: 4
Cooking Time: 25 Minutes
Ingredients:
- 1 cup refried beans
- 2 cups cheddar shreds
- ½ jalapeño pepper, minced
- ¼ chopped white onion
- 1 tsp oregano
- 15 soft corn tortillas

Directions:
1. Preheat air fryer at 350°F. Spread refried beans, jalapeño pepper, white onion, oregano and cheddar shreds down the center of each corn tortilla. Roll each tortilla tightly. Place tacos, seam side down, in the frying basket, and Air Fry for 4 minutes. Serve immediately.

Basil Green Beans

Servings: 4
Cooking Time: 15 Minutes
Ingredients:
- 1 ½ lb green beans, trimmed
- 1 tbsp olive oil
- 1 tbsp fresh basil, chopped
- Garlic salt to taste

Directions:
1. Preheat air fryer to 400°F. Coat the green beans with olive oil in a large bowl. Combine with fresh basil powder and garlic salt. Put the beans in the frying basket and Air Fry for 7-9 minutes, shaking once until the beans begin to brown. Serve warm and enjoy!

Home-style Cinnamon Rolls

Servings: 4
Cooking Time: 40 Minutes
Ingredients:
- ½ pizza dough
- 1/3 cup dark brown sugar
- ¼ cup butter, softened
- ½ tsp ground cinnamon

Directions:
1. Preheat air fryer to 360°F. Roll out the dough into a rectangle. Using a knife, spread the brown sugar and butter, covering all the edges, and sprinkle with cinnamon. Fold the long side of the dough into a log, then cut it into 8 equal pieces, avoiding compression. Place the rolls, spiral-side up, onto a parchment-lined sheet. Let rise for 20 minutes. Grease the rolls with cooking spray and Bake for 8 minutes until golden brown. Serve right away.

Cheesy Veggie Frittata

Servings: 2
Cooking Time: 65 Minutes
Ingredients:
- 4 oz Bella mushrooms, chopped
- ¼ cup halved grape tomatoes
- 1 cup baby spinach
- 1/3 cup chopped leeks
- 1 baby carrot, chopped
- 4 eggs
- ½ cup grated cheddar
- 1 tbsp milk
- ¼ tsp garlic powder
- ¼ tsp dried oregano
- Salt and pepper to taste

Directions:
1. Preheat air fryer to 300°F. Crack the eggs into a bowl and beat them with a fork or whisk. Mix in the remaining ingredients until well combined. Pour into a greased cake pan. Put the pan into the frying basket and Bake for 20-23 minutes or until eggs are set in the center. Remove from the fryer. Cut into halves and serve.

Party Giant Nachos

Servings: 2
Cooking Time: 20 Minutes
Ingredients:
- 2 tbsp sour cream
- ½ tsp chili powder
- Salt to taste
- 2 soft corn tortillas
- 2 tsp avocado oil
- ½ cup refried beans
- ¼ cup cheddar cheese shreds
- 2 tbsp Parmesan cheese
- 2 tbsp sliced black olives
- ¼ cup torn iceberg lettuce
- ¼ cup baby spinach
- ½ sliced avocado
- 1 tomato, diced
- 2 lime wedges

Directions:
1. Preheat air fryer at 400°F. Whisk the sour cream, chili powder, and salt in a small bowl. Brush tortillas with avocado oil and season one side with salt. Place tortillas in the frying basket and Bake for 3 minutes. Set aside.
2. Layer the refried beans, Parmesan and cheddar cheeses in the tortillas. Place them back into the basket and Bake for 2 minutes. Divide tortillas into 2 serving plates. Top each tortilla with black olives, baby spinach, lettuce, and tomatoes. Dollop sour cream mixture on each. Serve with lime and avocado wedges on the side.

Garlicky Roasted Mushrooms

Servings: 4
Cooking Time: 30 Minutes
Ingredients:
- 16 garlic cloves, peeled
- 2 tsp olive oil
- 16 button mushrooms
- 2 tbsp fresh chives, snipped
- Salt and pepper to taste
- 1 tbsp white wine

Directions:
1. Preheat air fryer to 350°F. Coat the garlic with some olive oil in a baking pan, then Roast in the air fryer for 12 minutes. When done, take the pan out and stir in the mushrooms, salt, and pepper. Then add the remaining olive oil and white wine. Put the pan back into the fryer and Bake for 10-15 minutes until the mushrooms and garlic soften. Sprinkle with chives and serve warm.

Quick-to-make Quesadillas

Servings: 4
Cooking Time: 30 Minutes
Ingredients:

- 12 oz goat cheese
- 2 tbsp vinegar
- 1 tbsp Taco seasoning
- 1 ripe avocado, pitted
- 4 scallions, finely sliced
- 2 tbsp lemon juice
- 4 flour tortillas
- ¼ cup hot sauce
- ½ cup Alfredo sauce
- 16 cherry tomatoes, halved

Directions:
1. Preheat air fryer to 400°F. Slice goat cheese into 4 pieces. Set aside. In a bowl, whisk vinegar and taco seasoning until combined. Submerge each slice into the vinegar and Air Fry for 12 minutes until crisp, turning once. Let cool slightly before cutting into 1/2-inch thick strips.
2. Using a fork, mash the avocado in a bowl. Stir in scallions and lemon juice and set aside. Lay one tortilla on a flat surface, cut from one edge to the center, then spread ¼ of the avocado mixture on one quadrant, 1 tbsp of hot sauce on the next quadrant, and finally 2 tbsp of Alfredo sauce on the other half. Top the non-sauce half with ¼ of cherry tomatoes and ¼ of goat cheese strips.
3. To fold, start with the avocado quadrant, folding each over the next one until you create a stacked triangle. Repeat the process with the remaining tortillas. Air Fry for 5 minutes until crispy, turning once. Serve warm.

General Tso's Cauliflower

Servings: 4
Cooking Time: 15 Minutes
Ingredients:

- 1 head cauliflower cut into florets
- ¾ cup all-purpose flour, divided
- 3 eggs, lightly beaten
- 1 cup panko breadcrumbs*
- canola or peanut oil, in a spray bottle
- 2 tablespoons oyster sauce
- ¼ cup soy sauce
- 2 teaspoons chili paste
- 2 tablespoons rice wine vinegar
- 2 tablespoons sugar
- ¼ cup water
- white or brown rice for serving
- steamed broccoli

Directions:
1. Set up dredging station using three bowls. Place the cauliflower in a large bowl and sprinkle ¼ cup of the flour over the top. Place the eggs in a second bowl and combine the panko breadcrumbs and remaining ½ cup flour in a third bowl. Toss the cauliflower in the flour to coat all the florets thoroughly. Dip the cauliflower florets in the eggs and finally toss them in the breadcrumbs to coat on all sides. Place the coated cauliflower florets on a baking sheet and spray generously with canola or peanut oil.
2. Preheat the air fryer to 400°F.
3. Air-fry the cauliflower at 400°F for 15 minutes, flipping the florets over for the last 3 minutes of the cooking process and spraying again with oil.
4. While the cauliflower is air-frying, make the General Tso Sauce. Combine the oyster sauce, soy sauce, chili paste, rice wine vinegar, sugar and water in a saucepan and bring the mixture to a boil on the stove top. Lower the heat and let it simmer for 10 minutes, stirring occasionally.
5. When the timer is up on the air fryer, transfer the cauliflower to a large bowl, pour the sauce over it all and toss to coat. Serve with white or brown rice and some steamed broccoli.

Vegetable Side Dishes Recipes
Cheddar Tomatillos With Lettuce

Servings: 4
Cooking Time: 4 Minutes
Ingredients:
- 2 tomatillos
- ¼ cup coconut flour
- 2 eggs, beaten
- ¼ teaspoon ground nutmeg
- ¼ teaspoon chili flakes
- 1 ounce Cheddar cheese, shredded
- 4 lettuce leaves

Directions:
1. Cut the tomatillos into slices.
2. Mix ground nutmeg, chili flakes, and beaten eggs in a bowl.
3. Brush the tomatillo slices with the egg mixture. Then coat with coconut flour.
4. Repeat above steps with the rest slices.
5. Before cooking, heat your air fryer to 400 degrees F/ 205 degrees C.
6. Place the coated tomatillo slices in the air fryer basket in a single layer.
7. Cook in your air fryer for 2 minutes from each side.
8. When cooked, add the lettuce leaves on the top of the tomatillos.
9. To serve, sprinkle with shredded cheese.

Potato With Creamy Cheese

Servings:2
Cooking Time: 15 Minutes
Ingredients:
- 2 medium potatoes
- 1 teaspoon butter
- 3 tablespoons sour cream
- 1 teaspoon chives
- 1½ tablespoons grated Parmesan cheese

Directions:
1. Preheat the air fryer to 350ºF (177ºC).
2. Pierce the potatoes with a fork and boil them in water until they are cooked.
3. Transfer to the air fryer and air fry for 15 minutes.
4. In the meantime, combine the sour cream, cheese and chives in a bowl. Cut the potatoes halfway to open them up and fill with the butter and sour cream mixture.
5. Serve immediately.

Balsamic Brussels Sprouts

Servings: 6
Cooking Time: 10 Minutes
Ingredients:
- 2 cups Brussels sprouts, sliced
- 1 tablespoon balsamic vinegar
- 1 tablespoon olive oil
- ¼ teaspoon salt

Directions:
1. Add all the recipe ingredients into the suitable bowl and toss well.
2. Grease its air fryer basket with cooking spray.
3. Transfer Brussels sprouts mixture into the air fryer basket.
4. Cook Brussels sprouts at 400 degrees F/ 205 degrees C for almost 10 minutes. Shake basket halfway through.
5. Serve and enjoy.

Roasted Brown Butter Carrots

Servings: 4
Cooking Time: 20 Minutes
Ingredients:
- 1 tablespoon unsalted butter
- 6 carrots, cut into ½-inch pieces (about 3 cups)
- Salt
- Pepper

Directions:
1. Place a saucepan over high heat. Add the butter. Allow the butter to melt for 2 to 3 minutes.
2. Stirring constantly to ensure it does not scorch, cook for 1 to 2 minutes, until it starts to turn brown. Brown bits will form on the bottom of the pan. Remove the pan from heat.
3. In a large bowl, combine the carrots with the brown butter. Season with salt and pepper to taste.
4. Transfer the carrots to the air fryer. Cook for 6 minutes.
5. Open the air fryer and shake the basket. Cook for an additional 6 minutes.
6. Cool before serving.

Air Fried Brussels Sprouts

Servings: 4
Cooking Time: 20 Minutes

Ingredients:
- 1 pound Brussels sprouts, trimmed and halved
- Black pepper and salt to the taste
- 2 tablespoons ghee, melted
- ½ cup coconut cream
- 2 tablespoons. garlic, minced
- 1 tablespoon chives, chopped

Directions:
1. In your air fryer, mix the sprouts with the rest of the ingredients except the chives, toss well, introduce in the preheated air fryer and cook them at 370 degrees F/ 185 degrees C for 20 minutes.
2. Divide the Brussels sprouts between plates, sprinkle the chives on top and serve as a side dish.

Spiced Cauliflower Medley

Servings: 4
Cooking Time: 15 Minutes

Ingredients:
- 1 pound cauliflower florets, roughly grated
- 3 eggs, whisked
- 3 tablespoons butter, melted
- Salt and black pepper to the taste
- 1 tablespoon sweet paprika

Directions:
1. Set heat to high and then melt the butter in a pan.
2. Then add the cauliflower in the pan and cook until brown for 5 minutes.
3. Add salt, the whisked eggs, paprika, and pepper. Toss well.
4. Cook in your air fryer at 400 degrees F/ 205 degrees C for 10 minutes.
5. Serve on plates.

Herbed Radishes

Servings: 2
Cooking Time: 10 Minutes

Ingredients:
- 1 pound (454 g) radishes
- 2 tablespoons unsalted butter, melted
- ¼ teaspoon dried oregano
- ½ teaspoon dried parsley
- ½ teaspoon garlic powder

Directions:
1. Preheat the air fryer to 350°F (177°C). Prepare the radishes by cutting off their tops and bottoms and quartering them.
2. In a bowl, combine the butter, dried oregano, dried parsley, and garlic powder. Toss with the radishes to coat.
3. Transfer the radishes to the air fryer and air fry for 10 minutes, shaking the basket at the halfway point to ensure the radishes air fry evenly through. The radishes are ready when they turn brown.
4. Serve immediately.

Garlic Brussel Sprouts With Celery

Servings: 6
Cooking Time: 13 Minutes

Ingredients:
- 1 pound Brussels sprouts
- 1 teaspoon minced garlic
- 2 ounces celery stalks, minced
- 1 tablespoon butter, melted
- 1 teaspoon cayenne pepper
- ¼ teaspoon salt

Directions:
1. Roughly chop the Brussels sprouts with celery, cayenne pepper, butter, salt, and minced garlic.
2. Shake the mixture and marinate for 10 minutes.
3. Before cooking, heat the air fryer to 385 degrees F/ 195 degrees C.
4. Cook the marinated Brussels sprouts in your air fryer for 13 minutes.
5. During cooking, shake the basket from time to time.

Lush Summer Rolls

Servings: 4
Cooking Time: 15 Minutes

Ingredients:
- 1 cup shiitake mushroom, sliced thinly
- 1 celery stalk, chopped
- 1 medium carrot, shredded
- ½ teaspoon finely chopped ginger
- 1 teaspoon sugar
- 1 tablespoon soy sauce
- 1 teaspoon nutritional yeast
- 8 spring roll sheets
- 1 teaspoon corn starch
- 2 tablespoons water

Directions:
1. In a bowl, combine the ginger, soy sauce, nutritional yeast, carrots, celery, mushroom, and sugar.
2. Mix the cornstarch and water to create an adhesive for the spring rolls.
3. Scoop a tablespoonful of the vegetable mixture into the middle of the spring roll sheets. Brush the edges of the sheets with the cornstarch adhesive and enclose around the filling to make spring rolls.
4. Preheat the air fryer to 400°F (204°C). When warm, place the rolls inside and air fry for 15 minutes or until crisp.
5. Serve hot.

Parmesan Green Beans

Servings: 4
Cooking Time: 7 Minutes

Ingredients:
- Olive oil
- 1 cup whole-wheat panko bread crumbs
- ¼ cup grated Parmesan cheese
- 1 teaspoon garlic powder
- ½ teaspoon freshly ground black pepper
- ½ teaspoon salt
- 1 egg
- 1 pound fresh green beans, trimmed

Directions:
1. Spray a fryer basket lightly with olive oil.
2. In a medium bowl, mix together the panko bread crumbs, Parmesan cheese, garlic powder, black pepper, and salt.
3. In a small, shallow bowl, whisk the egg.
4. Dip the green beans in the whisked egg and then coat in the panko bread crumb mixture.
5. Place the green beans in a single layer in the fryer basket. Spritz lightly with olive oil. You may need to cook more than one batch.
6. Air fry until light brown and crispy, 5 to 7 minutes.

Roasted Eggplant Slices

Servings: 1
Cooking Time: 15 Minutes
Ingredients:
- 1 large eggplant, sliced
- 2 tablespoons olive oil
- ¼ teaspoon salt
- ½ teaspoon garlic powder

Directions:
1. Preheat the air fryer to 390°F (199°C).
2. Apply the olive oil to the slices with a brush, coating both sides. Season each side with sprinklings of salt and garlic powder.
3. Put the slices in the air fryer and roast for 15 minutes.
4. Serve immediately.

Crunchy Green Beans

Servings: 4
Cooking Time: 10 Minutes
Ingredients:
- 1½ pounds green beans, trimmed
- 1 tablespoon extra-virgin olive oil
- 1 teaspoon garlic powder
- Salt
- Pepper

Directions:
1. In a large bowl, drizzle the green beans with the olive oil. Sprinkle with the garlic powder and salt and pepper to taste. Mix well.
2. Transfer the green beans to the air fryer basket. Cook for 4 minutes.
3. Open the air fryer and shake the basket. Cook for an additional 3 to 4 minutes, until the green beans have turned slightly brown.
4. Cool before serving.

Crispy Broccoli

Servings: 4
Cooking Time: 11 Minutes
Ingredients:
- 1 large head fresh broccoli
- 2 teaspoons olive oil
- 1 tablespoon lemon juice

Directions:
1. Rinse the broccoli and pat dry. Cut off the florets and separate them. You can use the stems of the broccoli too; cut them into 1″ chunks and peel them.
2. Toss the broccoli, olive oil, and lemon juice in a large bowl until coated.
3. Roast the broccoli, in batches, for 10 to 14 minutes or until the broccoli is crisp-tender and slightly brown around the edges. Repeat with the remaining broccoli. Serve immediately.

Italian Eggplant And Tomato Bites

Servings: 5
Cooking Time: 10 Minutes
Ingredients:
- 2 medium eggplants, trimmed
- 1 tomato
- 1 teaspoon Italian seasonings
- 1 teaspoon avocado oil
- 3 ounces Parmesan, sliced

Directions:
1. Cut the eggplants into 5 slices and thinly slice the tomato into 5 slices.
2. Transfer the eggplant slices in the air fryer basket in a single layer.
3. Cook in your air fryer at 400 degrees F/ 205 degrees C for 3 minutes from each side.
4. Then top the eggplants with tomato slices.
5. Season with avocado oil and Italian seasonings.
6. Sprinkle on top with Parmesan.
7. Cook in your air fryer at 400 degrees F/ 205 degrees C for 4 minutes.

Garlic Kale Mash

Servings: 4
Cooking Time: 20 Minutes
Ingredients:
- 1 cauliflower head, florets separated
- 4 teaspoons butter, melted
- 4 garlic cloves, minced
- 3 cups kale, chopped
- 2 scallions, chopped
- A pinch of black pepper and salt
- ⅓ cup coconut cream
- 1 tablespoon parsley, chopped

Directions:
1. In a pan that fits the air fryer, combine the cauliflower with the butter, garlic, scallions, salt, black pepper and the cream, toss, introduce the pan in the machine and cook at almost 380 degrees F/ 195 degrees C for 20 minutes.
2. Mash the mix well, add the remaining ingredients, whisk, divide between plates and serve.

Parmesan Zucchini Gratin

Servings: 2
Cooking Time: 15 Minutes
Ingredients:
- 5 ounces parmesan cheese, shredded
- 1 tablespoon coconut flour
- 1 tablespoon dried parsley
- 2 zucchinis
- 1 teaspoon butter, melted

Directions:
1. In a bowl, add the coconut flour and parmesan cheese together.
2. To season, add parsley.
3. Cut the zucchinis lengthwise in half and slice the halves into four slices.
4. Before cooking, heat your air fryer to 400 degrees F/ 205 degrees C.
5. Then coat the zucchinis with the melted butter and dip in the parmesan-flour mixture to thoroughly coat the zucchini slices.
6. Cook in your air fryer for 13 minutes.

Spicy Sweet Potatoes

Servings: 4
Cooking Time: 15 Minutes
Ingredients:
- Olive oil
- 1½ teaspoon salt
- 1 teaspoon chili powder
- 1 teaspoon paprika
- 1 teaspoon onion powder
- ½ teaspoon ground cumin
- ½ teaspoon freshly ground black pepper
- ¼ teaspoon cayenne pepper
- 2 large sweet potatoes, peeled and cut into 1-inch pieces

Directions:
1. Spray a fryer basket lightly with olive oil.
2. In a small bowl, combine the salt, chili powder, paprika, onion powder, cumin, black pepper, and cayenne pepper.
3. In a large bowl, add the sweet potato and spray lightly with olive oil. Add the seasoning mix and toss to coat.
4. Put the sweet potatoes in the fryer basket. Air fry until browned and slightly crispy, about 15 minutes, shaking the basket every 5 minutes and spraying lightly with olive oil each time. To make them extra crispy, cook for a few more minutes but watch closely to make sure they don't burn.

Balsamic Greens And Green Beans Medley

Servings: 4
Cooking Time: 12 Minutes
Ingredients:
- 1 bunch mustard greens, trimmed
- 1-pound green beans, halved
- 2 tablespoons olive oil
- ¼ cup keto tomato sauce
- 3 garlic cloves, minced
- Black pepper and salt to the taste
- 1 tablespoon balsamic vinegar

Directions:
1. In a suitable pan that fits your air fryer, mix the mustard greens with the rest of the ingredients, toss, put the pan in the air fryer and cook them together in your air fryer for 12 minutes at almost 350 degrees F/ 175 degrees C.
2. Divide everything between plates and serve.

Yellow Squash Chips With Parmesan

Servings: 4
Cooking Time: 10 Minutes
Ingredients:
- ½ cup flour
- Black pepper and salt to taste
- 2 eggs
- 1 tablespoon soy sauce
- ¾ cup panko breadcrumbs
- 1 tablespoon dried dill
- ¼ cup Parmesan cheese, grated
- Greek yogurt dressing, for serving

Directions:
1. At 380 degrees F/ 195 degrees C, preheat your Air fryer.
2. Grease its air fryer basket with cooking spray.
3. In a suitable bowl, mix the flour, dill, salt, and black pepper.
4. In another bowl, beat the eggs with soy sauce. In a third, pour the panko breadcrumbs and Parmesan cheese.
5. Dip the squash rounds in the flour, then in the eggs, and then coat with the breadcrumbs.
6. Place in the air fryer basket.
7. Cook for almost 10 minutes, flipping once halfway through.
8. Serve with Greek yogurt dressing.

Zucchini Tots With Mozzarella

Servings: 4
Cooking Time: 6 Minutes
Ingredients:
- 1 zucchini, grated
- ½ cup Mozzarella, shredded
- 1 egg, beaten
- 2 tablespoons. almond flour
- ½ teaspoon black pepper
- 1 teaspoon coconut oil, melted

Directions:
1. Mix up grated zucchini, shredded Mozzarella, egg, almond flour, and black pepper.
2. Then make the small zucchini tots with the help of the fingertips.
3. At 385 degrees F/ 195 degrees C, preheat your air fryer.
4. Place the zucchini tots in the air fryer basket and cook for 3 minutes from each side or until the zucchini tots are golden brown.
5. Serve.

Roasted "everything Bagel" Broccolini

Servings: 4
Cooking Time: 12 Minutes

Ingredients:

- 1½ teaspoons olive oil, plus more for spraying
- 1 pound broccolini
- 1 tablespoon everything bagel seasoning

Directions:

1. Spray the fryer basket lightly with olive oil.
2. In a large bowl, toss the broccolini with the ½ tablespoon olive oil and everything bagel seasoning.
3. Place the broccolini in the fryer basket in a single layer. You may need to cook them in batches.
4. Air fry until the broccolini are tender and lightly browned, 8 to 12 minutes, making sure to shake the basket after 5 minutes of cooking. Repeat with any remaining broccolini.

Black Bean And Tomato Chili

Servings: 6
Cooking Time: 23 Minutes

Ingredients:

- 1 tablespoon olive oil
- 1 medium onion, diced
- 3 garlic cloves, minced
- 1 cup vegetable broth
- 3 cans black beans, drained and rinsed
- 2 cans diced tomatoes
- 2 chipotle peppers, chopped
- 2 teaspoons cumin
- 2 teaspoons chili powder
- 1 teaspoon dried oregano
- ½ teaspoon salt

Directions:

1. Over a medium heat, fry the garlic and onions in the olive oil for 3 minutes.
2. Add the remaining ingredients, stirring constantly and scraping the bottom to prevent sticking.
3. Preheat the air fryer to 400°F (204°C).
4. Take a dish and place the mixture inside. Put a sheet of aluminum foil on top.
5. Transfer to the air fryer and bake for 20 minutes.
6. When ready, plate up and serve immediately.

Desserts And Sweets Recipes

Choco Chips Cookies With Macadamia Nuts

Servings:4
Cooking Time: 15 Minutes

Ingredients:
- 1 egg
- 3 tablespoons butter
- 1 teaspoon vanilla
- ¼ teaspoon baking powder
- 2 tablespoons macadamia nuts, crushed
- 1 cup almond flour
- 2 tablespoons unsweetened chocolate chips
- Pinch of salt

Directions:
1. In a suitable bowl, beat egg using a hand mixer.
2. Stir in almond flour, butter, vanilla, baking powder, and salt and stir well.
3. Add Chocó chips and macadamia nuts and mix until dough is formed.
4. At 360 degrees F/ 180 degrees C, preheat your air fryer.
5. Make cookies from dough and place into the air fryer and cook for almost 15 minutes.
6. Serve and enjoy.

Graham Cracker Cheesecake

Servings:8
Cooking Time: 20 Minutes

Ingredients:
- 1 cup graham cracker crumbs
- 3 tablespoons softened butter
- 1½ (8-ounce / 227-g) packages cream cheese, softened
- ⅓ cup sugar
- 2 eggs
- 1 tablespoon flour
- 1 teaspoon vanilla
- ¼ cup chocolate syrup

Directions:
1. For the crust, combine the graham cracker crumbs and butter in a small bowl and mix well. Press into the bottom of a baking pan and put in the freezer to set.
2. For the filling, combine the cream cheese and sugar in a medium bowl and mix well. Beat in the eggs, one at a time. Add the flour and vanilla.
3. Preheat the air fryer to 450ºF (232ºC).
4. Remove ⅔ cup of the filling to a small bowl and stir in the chocolate syrup until combined.
5. Pour the vanilla filling into the pan with the crust. Drop the chocolate filling over the vanilla filling by the spoonful. With a clean butter knife, stir the fillings in a zigzag pattern to marbleize them.
6. Bake for 20 minutes or until the cheesecake is just set.
7. Cool on a wire rack for 1 hour, then chill in the refrigerator until the cheesecake is firm.
8. Serve immediately.

Chocolate-almond Candies

Servings: 4
Cooking Time: 2 Minutes
Ingredients:
- 1-ounce almonds, crushed
- 1-ounce dark chocolate
- 2 tablespoons peanut butter
- 2 tablespoons heavy cream

Directions:
1. At 390 degrees F/ 200 degrees C, preheat your air fryer.
2. Chop the dark chocolate bar and put it in the preheated air fryer mold.
3. Add peanut butter and heavy cream.
4. Stir the mixture and transfer in the air fryer.
5. Cook it for 2 minutes or until it starts to be melt.
6. Then line the air fryer tray with parchment.
7. Put the crushed almonds on the tray in 1 layer.
8. Then pour the cooked chocolate mixture over the almonds.
9. Flatten gently if needed and let it cool.
10. Crack the cooked chocolate layer into the candies.

Sweet Orange Muffins

Servings: 5
Cooking Time: 10 Minutes
Ingredients:
- 5 eggs, beaten
- 1 tablespoon poppy seeds
- 1 teaspoon vanilla extract
- ¼ teaspoon ground nutmeg
- ½ teaspoon baking powder
- 1 teaspoon orange juice
- 1 teaspoon orange zest, grated
- 5 tablespoons coconut flour
- 1 tablespoon Monk fruit
- 2 tablespoons coconut flakes
- Cooking spray

Directions:
1. After adding the eggs, poppy seeds, vanilla extract, ground nutmeg, baking powder, orange juice, orange zest, coconut flour, Monk fruit and coconut flakes, mix them well until homogenous and have no clumps.
2. Spray the inside of the muffin molds.
3. Pour the mixture batter in the molds and then arrange them to the air fryer.
4. Cook them at 360 degrees F/ 180 degrees C for 10 minutes.
5. When cooked, serve and enjoy.

Chocolate Almond Cake

Servings: 4
Cooking Time: 15 Minutes
Ingredients:
- 1½ tablespoons almond flour
- 3½ ounces unsalted butter
- 3½ ounces sugar free dark chocolate, chopped
- 2 eggs
- 3½ tablespoons swerve

Directions:
1. At 375 degrees F/ 190 degrees C, preheat your air fryer. and grease 4 regular sized ramekins.
2. Microwave all chocolate bits with butter in a suitable bowl for about 3 minutes.
3. Remove this melt from the microwave and whisk in the eggs and swerve.
4. Add the flour and mix well until smooth.
5. Transfer the mixture into the ramekins and arrange in the air fryer basket.
6. Cook for about 10 minutes and dish out to serve.

Chocolate Croissants

Servings: 8
Cooking Time: 24 Minutes
Ingredients:
- 1 sheet frozen puff pastry, thawed
- ⅓ cup chocolate-hazelnut spread
- 1 large egg, beaten

Directions:
1. On a lightly floured surface, roll puff pastry into a 14-inch square. Cut pastry into quarters to form 4 squares. Cut each square diagonally to form 8 triangles.
2. Spread 2 teaspoons chocolate-hazelnut spread on each triangle; from wider end, roll up pastry. Brush egg on top of each roll.
3. Preheat the air fryer to 375ºF (191ºC). Air fry rolls in batches, 3 or 4 at a time, 8 minutes per batch, or until pastry is golden brown.
4. Cool on a wire rack; serve while warm or at room temperature.

Strawberry Muffins With Cinnamon

Servings: 12
Cooking Time: 15 Minutes
Ingredients:
- 3 eggs
- 1 teaspoon ground cinnamon
- 2 teaspoons baking powder
- 2 ½ cups almond flour
- ⅔ cup fresh strawberries, diced
- ⅓ cup heavy cream
- 1 teaspoon vanilla
- ½ cup Swerve
- 5 tablespoons butter

Directions:
1. Before cooking, heat your air fryer to 325 degrees F/ 160 degrees C.
2. In a bowl, add the sweetener and butter and use a hand mixer to beat until smooth.
3. Beat in cream, whisked eggs, and vanilla until frothy.
4. Sift the cinnamon, baking powder, salt, and almond flour together in a second bowl.
5. Mix the flour mixture together with the wet ingredients until well incorporated.
6. Then place the strawberries. Fold and press well.
7. Divide the batter into the silicone muffin molds.
8. Cook in batches in your air fryer at 325 degrees F/ 160 degrees C for 15 minutes.
9. Enjoy!

Black Forest Pies

Servings: 6
Cooking Time: 15 Minutes
Ingredients:
- 3 tablespoons milk or dark chocolate chips
- 2 tablespoons thick, hot fudge sauce
- 2 tablespoons chopped dried cherries
- 1 (10-by-15-inch) sheet frozen puff pastry, thawed
- 1 egg white, beaten
- 2 tablespoons sugar
- ½ teaspoon cinnamon

Directions:
1. Preheat the air fryer to 350ºF (177ºC).
2. In a small bowl, combine the chocolate chips, fudge sauce, and dried cherries.
3. Roll out the puff pastry on a floured surface. Cut into 6 squares with a sharp knife.
4. Divide the chocolate chip mixture into the center of each puff pastry square. Fold the squares in half to make triangles. Firmly press the edges with the tines of a fork to seal.
5. Brush the triangles on all sides sparingly with the beaten egg white. Sprinkle the tops with sugar and cinnamon.
6. Put in the air fryer basket and bake for 15 minutes or until the triangles are golden brown. The filling will be hot, so cool for at least 20 minutes before serving.

Mixed Berry Crumble

Servings: 4
Cooking Time:11 To 16 Minutes

Ingredients:
- ½ cup chopped fresh strawberries
- ½ cup fresh blueberries
- ⅓ cup frozen raspberries
- 1 tablespoon freshly squeezed lemon juice
- 1 tablespoon honey
- ⅔ cup whole-wheat pastry flour (see Tip)
- 3 tablespoons packed brown sugar
- 2 tablespoons unsalted butter, melted

Directions:
1. In a 6-by-2-inch pan, combine the strawberries, blueberries, and raspberries. Drizzle with the lemon juice and honey.
2. In a small bowl, mix the pastry flour and brown sugar.
3. Stir in the butter and mix until crumbly. Sprinkle this mixture over the fruit.
4. Bake for 11 to 16 minutes, or until the fruit is tender and bubbly and the topping is golden brown. Serve warm.

Berry Crumble

Servings:4
Cooking Time: 15 Minutes

Ingredients:
- For the Filling:
- 2 cups mixed berries
- 2 tablespoons sugar
- 1 tablespoon cornstarch
- 1 tablespoon fresh lemon juice
- For the Topping:
- ¼ cup all-purpose flour
- ¼ cup rolled oats
- 1 tablespoon sugar
- 2 tablespoons cold unsalted butter, cut into small cubes
- Whipped cream or ice cream (optional)

Directions:
1. Preheat the air fryer to 400°F (204°C).
2. For the filling: In a round baking pan, gently mix the berries, sugar, cornstarch, and lemon juice until thoroughly combined.
3. For the topping: In a small bowl, combine the flour, oats, and sugar. Stir the butter into the flour mixture until the mixture has the consistency of bread crumbs.
4. Sprinkle the topping over the berries.
5. Put the pan in the air fryer basket and air fry for 15 minutes. Let cool for 5 minutes on a wire rack.
6. Serve topped with whipped cream or ice cream, if desired.

Cinnamon And Pecan Pie

Servings: 4
Cooking Time: 25 Minutes
Ingredients:
- 1 pie dough
- ½ teaspoons cinnamon
- ¾ teaspoon vanilla extract
- 2 eggs
- ¾ cup maple syrup
- ⅛ teaspoon nutmeg
- 3 tablespoons melted butter, divided
- 2 tablespoons sugar
- ½ cup chopped pecans

Directions:
1. Preheat the air fryer to 370°F (188°C).
2. In a small bowl, coat the pecans in 1 tablespoon of melted butter.
3. Transfer the pecans to the air fryer and air fry for about 10 minutes.
4. Put the pie dough in a greased pie pan and add the pecans on top.
5. In a bowl, mix the rest of the ingredients. Pour this over the pecans.
6. Put the pan in the air fryer and bake for 25 minutes.
7. Serve immediately.

Buttery Shortbread Sticks

Servings: 10
Cooking Time: 22 Minutes
Ingredients:
- ⅓ cup caster sugar
- 1 2/3 cups plain flour
- ¾ cup butter

Directions:
1. In a suitable bowl, mix the sugar and flour.
2. Add the butter and stir until it makes a smooth dough.
3. Cut the dough into ten equal-sized sticks. With a fork, lightly prick the sticks.
4. Place the sticks into the lightly greased baking pan.
5. Set the cook time to 12 minutes.
6. At 355 degrees F/ 180 degrees C, preheat your air fryer.
7. Arrange the pan in preheat air fry basket and insert it in the air fryer.
8. Place the baking pan to cool for about 5-10 minutes.
9. Serve.

Aromatic Cup With Blondies

Servings: 1
Cooking Time: 15 Minutes
Ingredients:
- 1 egg, beaten
- 1 tablespoon peanut butter
- ½ teaspoon baking powder
- 1 teaspoon lemon juice
- ½ teaspoon vanilla extract
- 1 teaspoon Erythritol
- 2 tablespoons coconut flour

Directions:
1. In a cup, thoroughly mix up all of the ingredients until homogenous.
2. Arrange the cup with blondies to your air fryer and cook the mixture at 350 degrees F/ 175 degrees C for 15 minutes.
3. When done, serve and enjoy.

Fried Bananas With Chocolate Sauce

Servings: 6
Cooking Time: 10 Minutes
Ingredients:
- 1 large egg
- ¼ cup cornstarch
- ¼ cup plain bread crumbs
- 3 bananas, halved crosswise
- Cooking oil
- Chocolate sauce (see Ingredient tip)

Directions:
1. In a small bowl, beat the egg. In another bowl, place the cornstarch. Place the bread crumbs in a third bowl.
2. Dip the bananas in the cornstarch, then the egg, and then the bread crumbs.
3. Spray the air fryer basket with cooking oil.
4. Place the bananas in the basket and spray them with cooking oil. Cook for 5 minutes.
5. Open the air fryer and flip the bananas. Cook for an additional 2 minutes.
6. Transfer the bananas to plates. Drizzle the chocolate sauce over the bananas, and serve.

Donuts With Cardamom

Servings: 4
Cooking Time: 6 Minutes
Ingredients:
- 1 teaspoon ground cardamom
- ½ teaspoon ground cinnamon
- ½ teaspoon baking powder
- ½ cup coconut flour
- 1 tablespoon Erythritol
- 1 egg, beaten
- 1 tablespoon butter, softened
- ¼ teaspoon salt
- Cooking spray

Directions:
1. Thoroughly mix up the Erythritol, ground cinnamon and ground cardamom in a suitable bowl.
2. In another bowl, mix up the coconut flour, baking powder, egg, salt, and butter. Knead the non-sticky dough.
3. Roll up the dough and use the donut cutter to form 4 donuts.
4. Coat every donut with the cardamom mixture, then place the donuts in a warm place to let it rest for 10 minutes.
5. Spray the cooking basket of your air fryer with cooking spray and transfer the donuts on it.
6. Cook the donuts at 355 degrees F/ 180 degrees C for 6 minutes or until they are golden brown.
7. Sprinkle the remaining cardamom mixture on the hot donuts.
8. Enjoy!

Sweet Blackberry Cream

Servings: 6
Cooking Time: 20 Minutes
Ingredients:
- 2 cups blackberries
- Juice of ½ lemon
- 2 tablespoons water
- 1 teaspoon vanilla extract
- 2 tablespoons swerve

Directions:
1. In a suitable bowl, mix all the recipe ingredients and whisk well.
2. Divide this into 6 ramekins, put them in a preheated air fryer and cook at almost 340 degrees F/ 170 degrees C for 20 minutes.
3. Cool down and serve.

Enticing Cappuccino Muffins

Servings: 12
Cooking Time: 20 Minutes
Ingredients:
- 4 eggs
- 2 cups almond flour
- ½ teaspoon vanilla
- 1 teaspoon espresso powder
- ½ cup sour cream
- 1 teaspoon cinnamon
- 2 teaspoons baking powder
- ¼ cup coconut flour
- ½ cup Swerve
- ¼ teaspoon salt

Directions:
1. Before cooking, heat your air fryer to 325 degrees F/ 160 degrees C.
2. In a blender, mix together vanilla, espresso powder, eggs, and sour cream until smooth.
3. Then blend again with cinnamon, coconut flour, baking powder, salt, and sweetener until smooth.
4. Divide the batter into the silicone muffin molds.
5. Cook in batches in the preheated air fryer for 20 minutes.
6. Serve and enjoy!

Vanilla Bars With Sesame Seeds

Servings: 6
Cooking Time: 10 Minutes
Ingredients:
- 1 cup coconut flour
- 2 tablespoons coconut flakes
- 2 eggs, beaten
- 1 teaspoon baking powder
- ¼ cup Erythritol
- 1 teaspoon vanilla extract
- 1 tablespoon butter, softened
- 1 teaspoon sesame seeds
- Cooking spray

Directions:
1. In a suitable bowl, add the coconut flour, coconut flakes, eggs, baking powder, Erythritol, vanilla extract, and sesame seeds, then use a spoon to stir the mixture well until it is homogenous.
2. Roll up the dough into the square and cut into the bars.
3. Cook the coconut bars at 325 degrees F/ 160 degrees C for 10 minutes.
4. When done, serve and enjoy.

Spice Cookies

Servings: 4
Cooking Time: 12 Minutes

Ingredients:

- 4 tablespoons (½ stick) unsalted butter, at room temperature
- 2 tablespoons agave nectar
- 1 large egg
- 2 tablespoons water
- 2½ cups almond flour
- ½ cup sugar
- 2 teaspoons ground ginger
- 1 teaspoon ground cinnamon
- ½ teaspoon freshly grated nutmeg
- 1 teaspoon baking soda
- ¼ teaspoon kosher salt

Directions:

1. Preheat the air fryer to 325°F (163°C).
2. Line the bottom of the air fryer basket with parchment paper cut to fit.
3. In a large bowl using a hand mixer, beat together the butter, agave, egg, and water on medium speed until fluffy.
4. Add the almond flour, sugar, ginger, cinnamon, nutmeg, baking soda, and salt. Beat on low speed until well combined.
5. Roll the dough into 2-tablespoon balls and arrange them on the parchment paper in the basket. (They don't really spread too much, but try to leave a little room between them.) Bake for 12 minutes, or until the tops of cookies are lightly browned.
6. Transfer to a wire rack and let cool completely.
7. Serve immediately

Fried Oreos

Servings: 12 Cookies
Cooking Time: 20 Minutes

Ingredients:

- 12 Oreos or other chocolate sandwich cookies
- 1 cup of pancake and baking mix
- ¼ cup of milk
- 1 large egg
- 2 tablespoons of sugar
- 1 teaspoon of vanilla extract

Directions:

1. Cover the air fryer basket with a piece of parchment paper and spray some oil over it. Preheat your air fryer to 350°F.
2. Add the milk, vanilla, and egg in a medium bowl. Whisk it until mix. Add in the pancake mix and sugar, continue whisking. The batter consistency should be thick, just to coat the cookie.
3. Take 6 cookies and dip them in the prepared batter, wait until excess will drip back. Place the coated cookies in the preheated air fryer basket in a single layer. Avoid touching each other! Cook at 350°F for about 7 minutes until golden-brown.
4. Repeat the last step with the remaining part of the cookies.
5. Top with some powdered sugar. Serve and enjoy your Fried Oreos!

Cardamom And Vanilla Custard

Servings: 2
Cooking Time: 25 Minutes

Ingredients:
- 1 cup whole milk
- 1 large egg
- 2 tablespoons plus 1 teaspoon sugar
- ¼ teaspoon vanilla bean paste or pure vanilla extract
- ¼ teaspoon ground cardamom, plus more for sprinkling

Directions:
1. Preheat the air fryer to 350°F (177°C).
2. In a medium bowl, beat together the milk, egg, sugar, vanilla, and cardamom.
3. Put two ramekins in the air fryer basket. Divide the mixture between the ramekins. Sprinkle lightly with cardamom. Cover each ramekin tightly with aluminum foil. Bake for 25 minutes, or until a toothpick inserted in the center comes out clean.
4. Let the custards cool on a wire rack for 5 to 10 minutes.
5. Serve warm, or refrigerate until cold and serve chilled.

Caramelized Peaches With Blueberries

Servings: 6
Cooking Time: 7 To 11 Minutes

Ingredients:
- 3 peaches, peeled, halved, and pitted (see Tip)
- 2 tablespoons packed brown sugar
- 1 cup plain nonfat Greek yogurt
- 1 teaspoon pure vanilla extract
- ¼ teaspoon ground cinnamon
- 1 cup fresh blueberries

Directions:
1. Place the peaches, cut-side up, in the air fryer basket. Sprinkle evenly with the brown sugar. Bake for 7 to 11 minutes, or until they start to brown around the edges and become tender.
2. Meanwhile, in a small bowl, stir together the yogurt, vanilla, and cinnamon.
3. When the peaches are done, transfer them to a serving plate. Top with the yogurt mixture and the blueberries. Serve immediately.

Recipe Index

A

Air Fried Beef Ribs 55
Air Fried Brussels Sprouts 84
Air Fried Ribeye Steak 54
Air Fried Shrimp & Bacon 29
Apple Chips 26
Aromatic Cup With Blondies 99
Artichoke-spinach Dip 28
Authentic Greek Vegetable Skillet 46
Awesome Duck With Potato Rösti 42

B

Baked Eggs 15
Baked Potato Breakfast Boats 19
Baked Sardines 67
Balsamic Brussels Sprouts 83
Balsamic Greens And Green Beans Medley 90
Barbecued Baby Back Ribs 56
Basil Green Beans 78
Beef And Mushroom Calzones 53
Beef And Spinach Rolls 47
Beef Bites With Potatoes 50
Beef Steak Fingers 54
Beef With Spanish Rice Casserole 57
Beer Squid 66
Berry Crumble 97
Black Bean And Tomato Chili 92
Black Bean Empanadas 70
Black Bean Stuffed Potato Boats 72
Black Forest Pies 96
Breaded Artichoke Hearts 31
Breaded Homestyle Chicken Strips 40
Broccoli Cheddar Stuffed Potatoes 76
Broccoli-spinach Dip 23
Buffalo Breaded Cauliflower Bites 30

Buttery Shortbread Sticks 98

C

Cajun Lemon Branzino 59
Cajun Zucchini Chips 27
Caramelized Peaches With Blueberries 103
Cardamom And Vanilla Custard 103
Cheddar Bacon Frittata 18
Cheddar Bean Taquitos 78
Cheddar Tomatillos With Lettuce 82
Cheese Crusted Chops 47
Cheese Sticks With Coconut 33
Cheesy Beef Meatballs 55
Cheesy Chicken Tacos 37
Cheesy Enchilada Stuffed Baked Potatoes 71
Cheesy Pork Chops 51
Cheesy Veggie Frittata 79
Chicken & Mushroom Meatballs 37
Chicken And Vegetable Fajitas 39
Chicken Casserole With Almonds 18
Choco Chips Cookies With Macadamia Nuts 93
Chocolate Almond Cake 95
Chocolate Croissants 95
Chocolate-almond Candies 94
Cilantro-lime Fried Shrimp 63
Cinnamon And Pecan Pie 98
Clams With Spring Onions 62
Corn On The Cob 74
Corn With Coriander And Parmesan Cheese 30
Cranberry Beignets 15
Creamy Baked Sausage 20
Creamy Chicken Breasts With Jalapeno 42
Creamy Savory Salmon 60
Crispy Avocados With Pico De Gallo 73
Crispy Broccoli 88

Crispy Chicken And Pickles Sandwich 45

Crispy Chicken Cordon Bleu 44

Crispy Mustard Fried Leek 25

Crispy Old Bay Chicken Wings 31

Crispy Parmesan Asparagus 20

Crunchy Green Beans 87

D

Delectable Chaffles 27

Donuts With Cardamom 100

E

Easy Tandoori Chicken 43

Egg Soufflé With Mushroom And Broccoli 21

Enticing Cappuccino Muffins 101

Enticing Pork Meatballs 23

F

Fish Mania With Mustard 60

Flavor Moroccan Harissa Shrimp 58

French Toast Sticks With Strawberry Sauce 16

Fried Bacon Slices 28

Fried Bananas With Chocolate Sauce 99

Fried Oreos 102

G

Garlic Brussel Sprouts With Celery 85

Garlic Kale Mash 89

Garlic Shrimp 66

Garlicky Roasted Mushrooms 80

General Tso's Cauliflower 81

Glazed Fillets 64

Gorgeous Jalapeño Poppers 74

Graham Cracker Cheesecake 93

Grit And Ham Fritters 11

H

Hearty Blueberry Oatmeal 17

Hearty Salad 69

Herbed Radishes 85

Homemade And Delectable Pork Chops 48

Homemade Cherry Breakfast Tarts 16

Home-style Cinnamon Rolls 79

Honey Turkey Tenderloin 36

Honey-glazed Chicken Drumettes 24

I

Italian Chicken And Veggies 38

Italian Eggplant And Tomato Bites 88

Italian Lamb Chops With Avocado Mayo 51

J

Juicy Cheeseburger 46

K

Korean Short Ribs 50

L

Lemon Parmesan Chicken 36

Lemon-pepper Tilapia With Garlic Aioli 65

Lush Summer Rolls 86

M

Marjoram Chicken Drumsticks 35

Meatless Kimchi Bowls 73

Mixed Berry Crumble 97

Mixed Pepper Hash With Mozzarella Cheese 21

Mozzarella Chives Omelet 12

O

Old Bay Cod Fish Fillets 61

P

Paprika Zucchini Spread 19

Parmesan Chicken Wings 34

Parmesan Green Beans 86

Parmesan Sausage Egg Muffins 17

Parmesan Spinach Muffins 12

Parmesan Zucchini Gratin 89

Party Giant Nachos 80

Peppercorn Crusted Beef Tenderloin 52

Peppery Chicken Meatballs 32

Pesto Fish Finger Sandwich 63

Pizza Portobello Mushrooms 75

Pork Tenderloins 52

Potato Cheese Crusted Chicken 38

Potato With Creamy Cheese 82

Q

Quick-to-make Quesadillas 81

Quinoa Burgers With Feta Cheese And Dill 77

R

Red Snapper With Hot Chili Paste 65

Rice & Bean Burritos 69

Roasted "everything Bagel" Broccolini 92

Roasted Almonds With Paprika 25

Roasted Brown Butter Carrots 83

Roasted Buttery Cashews 29

Roasted Chicken And Vegetable Salad 44

Roasted Eggplant Slices 87

Root Veggie Chips With Herb Salt 22

S

Salmon Nachos 33

Salmon On Bed Of Fennel And Carrot 67

Salmon Patties 64

Sea Bream Fillet With Tomato Sauce 68

Sesame-glazed Salmon 58

Simple Pork Chops 48

Soufflé 14

Sourdough Croutons 13

Spice Chicken Pieces 35

Spice Chicken Wings With Parmesan Cheese 40

Spice Chicken With Broccoli 43

Spice Cookies 102

Spiced Catfish Fillets 62

Spiced Cauliflower Medley 84

Spicy Asian Chicken Thighs With Soy Sauce 34

Spicy Chickpeas 26

Spicy Sweet Potatoes 90

Spinach And Artichoke Dip Wontons 32

Spinach And Mushroom Mini Quiche 13

Steak Fajitas With Vegetables 49

Strawberry Muffins With Cinnamon 96

Sweet Blackberry Cream 100

Sweet Orange Muffins 94

Sweet Roasted Carrots 78

Sweet-and-sour Polish Sausage 56

T

Tasty Chicken Fajitas 41

Tasty Juicy Salmon 68

Tex-mex Turkey Burgers 41

Tomato And Mozzarella Bruschetta 14

Trimmed Mackerel With Spring Onions 61

Tuna And Fruit Kebabs 59

U

Unique Beef Cheeseburgers 49

V

Vanilla Bars With Sesame Seeds 101

Vegetarian Stuffed Bell Peppers 72

Y

Yellow Squash Chips With Parmesan 91

Yogurt Eggs With Chives 22

Z

Zucchini Tots With Mozzarella 91